D0853333

Also by Cait Flanders

The Year of Less: How I Stopped Shopping, Gave Away My Belongings, and Discovered Life Is Worth More Than Anything You Can Buy in a Store

Adventures IN Opting OUT

a field guide to leading an intentional life

CAIT FLANDERS

Little, Brown Spark
New York Boston London

Little, Brown Spark
Hachette Book Group
1290 Avenue of the Americas, New York, NY 10104
littlebrownspark.com

First Edition: September 2020

Little, Brown Spark is an imprint of Little, Brown and Company, a
division of Hachette Book Group, Inc. The Little, Brown Spark name and
logo are trademarks of Hachette Book Group, Inc.

The publisher is not responsible for websites (or their content) that are not
owned by the publisher.

Illustrations by Amanda Sandlin

ISBN 978-0-316-53694-3
LCCN 2020936620

10 9 8 7 6 5 4 3 2 1

LSC-C

Printed in the United States of America

To the staff at The Little Man Coffee Company in Cardiff,
Wales, who take care of everyone who walks through the door,
no matter where they are on their journey.

Contents

Prologue

Am I really going to do this? This was the question I had been asking myself for months. The idea seemed impossible when I first came up with it in the spring of 2018, while walking along the historic walls that surround York, England, with my friend Kate. By the time I returned home to Canada that summer, I knew I wanted to try. From there, I attempted to answer some of the other questions and concerns I had. Like, *What would my family and friends think? How would this affect my finances? Shouldn't I be doing "better things" with my money? Would this hurt my chances of finding a partner and being able to maintain a relationship? And what if it doesn't "work"?* I thought I had worked through each one and come up with all the answers I needed to move forward. But when I gave notice at the condo I had been renting for the previous two years, I wasn't certain it was the right decision. And a month later, when I moved the last of my belongings into the back of my sister's truck and watched her drive away, I still wondered if I was making a mistake.

It was November 25, 2018, and a relatively warm winter

morning in Squamish, British Columbia, Canada. I had woken up early to watch the last sunrise I would ever witness from my balcony. With coffee in hand, I stepped outside, looked past the tops of the trees, and focused my eyes on Mount Garibaldi in the distance—specifically, at its prominently pointy snow-covered tip, better known as Atwell Peak. As a kid, this is exactly how I (and probably most of us) drew mountains: with two slopes—one up, one down—connected by a pointed peak in the middle. A triangle with no base. If it was a winter scene that I was creating, I would add a little squiggly line near the top to represent snow. Of course, as I got older and traveled and explored more, I learned that most mountains look much softer. They have curves and rounded tops, and that was true of many of the other Coast Mountains. But not this one. From a distance, Garibaldi looks like the mountain of kids' dreams. Not surprisingly, then, Atwell is one of the most recognized peaks in the region, and I'd had the privilege of being able to look at it every day that it wasn't hidden by cloud coverage. As quickly as the sun began to rise, those clouds rolled back in—which typically signaled that rain or snow was on the way—and the mountaintop I loved was painted over with a brushstroke of gray.

Despite the color of the sky, the temperature stayed warm and precipitation held off all morning, which is all anyone can ask for when one decides to move in the winter—or really any time of year in the Pacific Northwest. Even without the good weather, though, this move was always going to be *physically* easier than all the ones I'd completed before it, because I was packing up the smallest number of belongings I'd ever owned. In the months before, I had sold things like my bookshelf and lamps, and given away some items to friends who needed them more than I did. After decluttering and getting rid of 75 percent of my belongings a few years earlier, I had almost no attachment to physical objects. A bed, a dresser, and the desk I'd made with my dad the year before were the only pieces of furniture I was keeping, along with a couch I was gifting to him. Those four things, along with six small boxes, my outdoor gear, a wall-length mirror, and a custom painting by my friend Amanda Sandlin, were all my sister and I had to pack up. Months of wondering, worrying, and planning, and the whole move took us only an hour.

What made this one *more* difficult was the fact that I wasn't moving into a new home. Instead, I was putting my belongings in storage in my dad's basement and for an indeterminate amount of time. After five years of being fairly transient, sometimes home for as few as four days per month, I had made the decision to attempt a fully nomadic lifestyle. One where I wouldn't have a permanent home, but would instead slowly travel full-time and try to create the feeling of home wherever I went.

To start, I booked a one-way ticket to London, England. On the surface, I knew this should've been exciting, but I was hesitant to let myself feel that way. Traveling long term sounds fun in theory, but I didn't make this decision quickly or with blind optimism. I had moved enough times in my life to know how long it could take to feel at home in a new space or to find community in a new city. And although I hadn't actually been to many countries, I had traveled enough to know how disruptive and unsettling it could be. So, that question I had been grappling with—*Am I really going to do this?* I didn't have an answer—or at least I didn't know how long I could do it. The only thing I knew was that it was going to be hard at times, because doing the opposite of what everyone around you is doing always is. *That* is a situation I had some experience with.

For most of my life, I had followed in other people's footsteps, the same way so many of us either do what is expected of us or follow the invisible but well-worn paths that lead to what is culturally "normal." Despite dreaming of moving to Toronto and launching a career in publishing, after I graduated from college, I followed my parents' lead and advice and started working for the government in my hometown, Victoria, BC. For the next five years, I stayed in a cycle of working Monday to Friday and drinking and doing drugs with friends on weekends. At some point, I was sold on the idea that renting an apartment by myself and filling it with all-new matching furniture and decor was important, and I used credit to pay for it all. I also "needed" a car, and got a loan to pay for that too.

To an outsider, it might have looked as though I had everything one could imagine a single woman in her twenties wanting. I had ticked all the boxes, climbed the grown-up ladder, and reached what I thought "success" was, all by the young age of twenty-five. This was the path so many of the people in my life were on, or wanted to be on, and they all seemed happy with their choices. I, however, felt trapped—weighed down, both physically and emotionally—by a job I didn't want, in a place I didn't want to be, and with habits that left me both hollow and broke. The aha moment or turning point for each of these things was different, ranging from finding myself maxed out financially (the worst point) to recognizing and accepting that I didn't want alcohol to be part of my life anymore (the most honest and humbling moment). With each one, I got to a place where I knew it was time to change direction and take a new path in life. And then, one by one, I decided to opt out.

First I stopped doing drugs, then I quit drinking, and then I paid off my debt, all in the span of two years. I left the government to work for a financial startup, and then I left the startup and became self-employed. I also moved a number of times (including to Toronto, which turned out not to be the right city for me) until I finally ended up in Squamish in 2016 (very much the right place for me). And whenever I had the money for it, I went on a trip by myself. Each decision scared me, but I slowly learned how to trust my gut, and I followed my curiosity to see where these new paths would take me.

Years later, I've opted out of so many things you would think I was used to living differently than everyone around me. But the truth is, the decision to leave Squamish and fully embrace my nomadic lifestyle in 2018 felt like the most difficult one to make. Compared to quitting drinking, which meant walking away from something that was negatively impacting my life, leaving a place I loved made no logical sense. I had been here for only two years. It wasn't enough time, and yet it *was* enough time for it to become my home. I had made friends here—good friends, women who had become more like sisters. I was part of the creative community, had joined a volunteer group, and had invested time learning about our local politics and the issues that mattered most as our little town continued to grow. Most of the adventure stories I've read or heard about start with the person being deeply unhappy with some part of their life, but that wasn't the case for me. I had done all the work and created a life I genuinely loved. It had taken a lot for me to get here, so I couldn't properly explain why I knew I had to leave—at least temporarily. I just knew it was my next step. But with no one in my life to look to as an example, I didn't know if it was even possible to travel and live this way. Furthermore, I wasn't just challenging what my family and friends might consider to be an acceptable way of life. This time, I was challenging my own thoughts and opinions—stories I had grown up hearing and came to believe about people who "couldn't settle down," as well as the theory that travelers would "have to figure things out eventually."

After my sister pulled away with her truck, I finished cleaning the condo and completed my walk-through inspection. But even when I handed over the keys to my landlord, I still knew I wasn't fully ready to say goodbye to this place, this town, this life I had made for myself. I was afraid of what I was walking away from. Scared I'd miss out on something that could happen, or that my relationships with the people here would change while I was gone. And unsure if now really was the right time. These were the same concerns I had before I stopped doing drugs, quit drinking, left jobs, started to work for myself, moved to new cities, moved again, traveled solo, traveled more, and even tried things as simple as removing certain foods from my diet and ditching various social media platforms. There is a cost to staying on one path, especially if it doesn't feel like the one you should be on. But there is also a cost to walking away and venturing into the unknown. The real question that was embedded in each one of my concerns was, *What price am I willing to pay?*

I didn't have the answers. I didn't know if it would work (or what "work" even meant, in the case of giving up my home to travel long term) or if I would be happy about my decision later. All I knew was that I was following my curiosity. My excitement about the possibilities finally weighed just a little more than my fears. It wasn't going to be easy, but I had prepared as best as I could, and now it was time to go. I *was* going to do this.

As I walked out to my car and looked back up at the mountains, I finally had the clarity to see that this wasn't just a decision. It was a mindset I had developed, and a process I had experienced through all of my adventures in opting out.

Introduction

"Did you lose anyone along the way?" This is the question that first sparked the idea for this book. If I had been asked only once or twice, it probably wouldn't have registered as important or a topic potentially worth writing about. After my first book, *The Year of Less*, was released in 2018, I did more than one hundred interviews in the first few months, along with nearly twenty promotional events. Most interviewers wanted to know what the people in my life had thought about the experiment I had written about—a yearlong shopping ban during which I also decluttered and donated the majority of my belongings. But in that book I also wrote about the early days of my sobriety, as well as what I had learned about my consumption tendencies overall. And at every event, at least one person asked a question along the lines of that first one: *What did your family say? How did your social life change? Did you lose any friends?*

After the fifth or sixth event, I spotted the trend and also recognized that I didn't like my initial answer. It wasn't dishonest. I shared the truth, which was that some of my relationships changed that year. But I was withholding the *full* truth, which was that I absolutely did lose a few people along the way. Of course I did. You will always leave someone or something behind when you decide to change paths in life. It didn't feel good to say that at later events. It was a more complicated response, but it was the most honest one I could give. Because the answers to questions about how to manage the ups and downs of trying to change your life are never as simple as you want them to be—not even when you're doing what's right for you. *Especially* when you're doing what's right for you.

There is a line I wrote in my first book that says, "Once you see the truth you can't unsee it." That's usually one of the things that happens, and it ultimately helps me make a decision to change paths in life. Like when I finally recognized that getting blackout drunk always resulted in me getting into troublesome situations. Or how, after an entire year of budgeting and not being happy with the numbers, I finally understood that my spending habits were holding me back from achieving my financial goals. In each of those examples, I could see the path I was on and where it was leading, and I knew it wasn't the one I wanted to keep going down. I saw the truth, and the idea that I should make a change was planted.

In this instance, though, spotting the trend in people's questions helped me see why so many others might be deciding *not* to change paths in their own lives. It's not just the fear of losing family or friends—though that's a very real fear, and one that will probably be actualized early on. (If we're going to be really honest in this book, we might as well start here.) It's fear in general. Fear of how you'll handle social situations, and how you'll connect with people. Fear of how changing paths will impact other areas of your life, such as your health or finances. Fear that it will be the wrong choice. Fear that you will "fail" or it won't "work." Fear of how it will impact your future. Fear of entering the unknown. From what I've experienced personally and heard from others, it doesn't matter if you're doing something as simple as quitting social media or as complex as moving to a new city or country. When you decide to step off the path you're on and go down a different one, it's scary.

It's especially scary when you don't have anyone to look to for guidance. By that, I don't just mean a support network. If you're open to talking with the people in your life about the change you want to make, you should be able to find at least one person who encourages your choice, even if they haven't made the same one. The hard part is *that:* when you don't have anyone in your life who has made the same choice as you. Who has also quit social media or moved to a new city or country. Who has decided not to drink alcohol anymore or has switched to a vegetarian diet or vegan lifestyle. Who has drastically changed their career or started to work for themselves. Who has decided to be the first person not to join the family business or do what their parents expected of them. Who has moved into an alternative housing situation or attempted to travel long term. Who has opened up a marriage or decided never to get married, or who has even considered one of the many forms of nontraditional relationships. Who has decided not to have kids. Who has gone against what is socially or culturally normal in some way and can openly discuss all the ups and downs with you. Who has actively chosen to brush up against the situations you will face when you decide to hike your own hike, so to speak. And who can tell you if it will work out or not. This last point is especially important, because even if you do find someone who has made a choice similar to yours, you will still have different experiences on your individual journeys.

Not only is it scary to go it alone; it's also scary to put yourself in a situation where you will stand out. To be the *first* person to attempt to live differently. To dare to want something different at all. And to try and potentially "fail" publicly. You might find that you are met with nothing but kindness and support throughout your own journey, but that hasn't been my experience. For every person who has been fully enthusiastic about a choice I've made, I would say I've crossed paths with at least four who were less than understanding. Or who were more than happy to point out the mistakes I've made and who have tried to shame me back to my old ways of living (which are really their ways of living, but we'll get into that later). So I know why it's scary to risk standing out. The fear of being alone is wired into us. Historically, if you decided to live differently from the way you were raised, your family of origin could literally reject you. This could lead to being isolated and having a difficult time trying to survive in the world. Even though our reality in developed countries isn't quite as harsh as that today, the fear of being shamed or rejected still stops us from doing so many things—including being true to ourselves.

For any or all of these reasons, we stick to what we know. We continue to go through the motions. We follow the clear paths and play it safe. But deep down, something doesn't feel right. We don't always know what it is at first, but it's there. And we try to ignore it. Consciously or subconsciously, we try to distract our minds and numb our feelings. We might do this by creating the life we think we are supposed to have. Or we work too much, drink or eat too much, shop too much, spend too much time staring into our screens, and so on, so we don't have to think about the life we are living. We avoid having tough conversations, don't express ourselves honestly, feel misunderstood or defensive, and watch our relationships grow distant or crumble as a result. We keep ourselves busy and do anything we can to avoid seeing the signs that are trying to point us in a different direction. Which means we are ignoring our truths, and not speaking up for ourselves around others. And it hurts us. It hurts our chances of fully understanding who we are and becoming more ourselves. And it hurts other people's chances of getting to know us and our chances of connecting with the world in a deep and meaningful way. All because we are too afraid to try.

But therein lies the solution: the word "try." What if you gave yourself permission to simply *try* going down the new path? To not pressure yourself to reach a specific goal, which only leads to the conclusion that you will either pass or fail, but to just try something new? What if you gave yourself the grace to stumble and make mistakes? To not have to do something "right" or perfectly, but to face the challenges, see what you're capable of, and discover who you will be on the other side? What if you let yourself change direction partway through, or change your mind and stop whenever you wanted or needed to? What if you didn't feel as though you had to stick to this decision for the rest of your life? What if you could go on an *adventure in opting out*? What if you could know that it will come with risks and uncertainty but also rewards and lessons that could change your life in ways you have never imagined? Does that sound a little less scary?

Introduction

This is a conversation that's been missing from the simple/intentional living space, but it's also one I don't see people having around lifestyle changes in general. The content is always so focused on how to follow the steps and make the change that it doesn't address the fact that there are real human beings involved in the process. Human beings who are going to have a very human experience when they decide to do the opposite of what everyone around them is doing. And nobody seems to be comfortable saying the truth, which is that it's going to be hard. You are going to question your decision and think about giving up. And you are going to lose people along the way. Instead, we throw around overly simplified statements like "Just let go!" and "Say no!" and "Lead by example!" and suggest that then everything will magically get better. In the long term, that can potentially be true. When you know what your values are, it's certainly easier to make decisions that align with them. But in my experience, it always gets harder and more complicated first. That's because these aren't just little changes or challenges with pass or fail grades. You're starting an adventure in opting out. Opting out from the family stories, expectations, and messages that told you who you should be and how you should live. And opting out from the stories you've told yourself about who you thought you should be. It's not easy to change those stories, or to step off the path you've been walking along and take a different one. There are a lot of challenges that come with it. And we are doing a huge disservice by not talking about this, and better preparing one another for the journey we are about to take. That's why I wrote this book.

Before you flip to the first section, I need you to know two things about me. The first is that I grew up with very strong messaging about how I should live my life. My parents and extended family essentially read us their rule books, as though the way they did things was the way my siblings and I should do things too. My dad had some particularly strong opinions on topics like our careers and money. Other things were passed down through behavior that was modeled for us. And I have to say that none of their messages were necessarily bad. I tried a lot of the things they suggested, or that my friends/coworkers did, and I walked down their paths for a period of time. And I was actually "good" at most of it. I was good at working for the government. I was good at shopping and creating a home that I felt comfortable in and that people wanted to visit. I was good at spending my money in general. I was good at socializing and partying. And I was really good at staying in my hometown and sticking to what I did well.

But I wasn't happy. Not *unhappy,* per se, because I don't always like that word or think happiness is a great way to measure our lives. I *wasn't at peace* with my choices—they didn't feel right, for a number of reasons—and I was ignoring all the signs that were trying to point to this truth. The fact that I was constantly finding myself bored and counting down the hours until I could leave work. Buying a lot of stuff that I would never use because I didn't know who I really was. Digging myself deeper into debt. Partying too much, and wasting time being hungover or coming down from a high. Overeating and gaining weight. Staying in unhealthy relationships and feeling deeply unworthy. Never getting ahead, or achieving any of the goals or realizing any of the dreams I had. And I was overwhelmed and anxious about something in every area of my life. I was ignoring myself and the voice within that told me I didn't want this life, that I wanted to live a different way.

Introduction

Because the messaging in my life had always been so strong, I genuinely didn't know that it was possible. I didn't know what a different way of living looked like, or how I could go about making it a reality. I was also afraid to tell people how I was feeling. I was afraid to be honest, because the most honest thing I could say was that I didn't want to do what anyone else in my life was doing. And I was afraid to say that out loud, partially because I didn't want to disappoint people or risk hurting their feelings by suggesting that what they were doing was wrong. I also didn't want to make mistakes and look stupid. More than anything, though, I was scared to be the odd one out. I didn't like myself very much back then, and I couldn't handle the thought of being alone in the world. And that fear meant I was subconsciously doing a lot of things I didn't really want to do, just so I could feel connected to people—even if we were ultimately connecting in all the wrong ways.

I was terrified to tell people about every single one of the changes I have wanted to make in my life. To share that I might even *attempt* to opt out of something. First, I was scared to tell my parents. Then my extended family. Then my friends. Up until the moment when I shared the idea with them, it was a little fantasy that occupied my mind. I could daydream about what it might be like to take a different path and what I might find as I traveled farther down it. Saying the words made it more real, and left me in the vulnerable position of being subjected to a lot of feedback—most of which I didn't ask for. Some people have been supportive of the choices I've made, but many haven't. I've lost friends. Shifted and ended relationships. And every other fear I've had has been actualized, at least once. I've made mistakes. Wasted some money.

Realized that things weren't working. Changed my direction or my mind. Probably looked foolish or flaky in a few people's eyes. And yet I have never regretted trying.

Every adventure in opting out has been worth it, because as soon as I walked away from something that wasn't working for me, I could finally hear my own voice. I learned something about who I was, what mattered to me, and how I wanted to show up in this world. I learned how to determine what my values were and how to live in alignment with them. I wrote my own rule book. The opt-outs themselves didn't magically make everything better. Quitting drinking didn't solve all my problems. Getting out of debt didn't make me a financial expert. Decluttering on its own didn't change all my consumption tendencies. You can walk away from something and never look back to learn anything about your relationship to it. The opt-out itself was never the quick fix. Embracing the full adventure of it is what has changed my life.

It helped me quiet the messaging in my head and learn how to listen to myself. It stripped away all my usual coping mechanisms and helped me learn how to navigate the world in a more open and honest way. It taught me how to be a beginner again. It helped me build confidence in myself and trust that I was resilient and could figure out how to deal with any situation I found myself in. It helped me become more self-aware, which is hard but so beneficial for me and everyone I have crossed paths with since. It helped me find causes I am genuinely passionate about and give back in a way that I never did before. It helped me build more intentional and meaningful relationships with people. And it helped me become more *myself.* Now I get to walk through this world as my full self and live an intentional life according to my own values. And I never could've imagined I would get here. Twenty-five-year-old Cait couldn't have dreamt this up. That doesn't mean it's always easy. Living this way means having to be more courageous and vulnerable, and it feels as though I'm stumbling around sometimes. But I'm happy to keep showing up and doing that work, because this way of life keeps leading me in a direction that is so much more fulfilling than where my original path was taking me.

The second thing I need you to know about me is that I wasn't very adventurous as a kid. Growing up in British Columbia meant growing up in nature's playground. No matter which direction you looked, there was always at least one element of the landscape that you could turn into an adventure. You could climb boulders and mountains. Ride up and down the countless trails available in each new season. Play hide-and-seek among the ancient giants in our forests. Dip your toes in the turquoise waters of glacier-fed rivers and lakes. Pop over to any one of the thousands of islands and see what it had to offer. Skimboard along the waves as they hit our beaches. And, with the warm protection of a wet suit, get off the coast and into the Pacific Ocean. Super, Natural British Columbia was the province's slogan for many years, followed by Best Place on Earth. It takes only one look at the coastline, forests, or mountain ranges to see that the province lives up to both.

I hate to admit that, despite having access to so much natural beauty and wonder, I saw the outdoors as a challenge instead of a place filled with endless opportunities. When my dad asked if I wanted to explore a new area, or grab a flashlight and crawl into the abandoned mine nearby, I usually said no. Then I would add the excuse that I was busy or tired, or claim that I'd hurt myself in some way or another. But the most honest thing I can say now, as an adult, is that I didn't have the confidence to try new things. To venture into the unknown and see what it might hold for me. I was afraid of taking a wrong step and looking stupid. Afraid of falling and actually hurting myself. Basically, I was afraid of being "bad" at the outdoors.

That's not to say I never spent time outside. I just stuck to the few places that were closest to home. I became a creature of habit, doing the same things over and over again. I would ride my bike through the lower trails of the mountain in our backyard. Climb into the space where the big oak tree behind my school had split and then curl up and read a book there. Swim in a couple of the lakes. And go down to one of the three beaches I loved to watch the sunrise or sunset over our little island. I knew what to expect in these places. I knew how to get there, what I would see, what I would do, and how I would get back home. I didn't care what else surrounded them. Whenever someone came along and so much as suggested that we take a different path or see what was around a bend, I would tell them to go ahead without me. "I'll wait here" could have been my childhood catchphrase — one that stayed with me until my late twenties. I was always waiting. Other people were living, and I was waiting.

It's hard to think about this now, as an adult. To imagine all the little moments in time when I could have seen and experienced more of the world around me. When a simple "Yes!" could have turned into an unexpected adventure and an opportunity to build up the confidence I lacked and so desperately needed in those years. When I could have stopped thinking that everything was so hard and understood that I had only one lifetime to explore this beautiful world. But it's important that I share this because I need you to know that I wasn't always as brave as I may seem now. Honestly, I'm still not sure that's a word I would use to describe myself. Despite what you might think when you read this book or look at my Instagram account, I still don't always love going on big outdoor adventures. And I don't always love it for the same reason I don't always love changing paths in life: because I know it's not going to be easy.

It wasn't until I quit drinking that I started hiking more regularly. Using my two feet (and occasionally my hands for help) to walk off the main roads and out into nature. And what I have come to learn in the years since is that there is an incredible parallel between taking a different path in life and the psychological work it takes to summit a mountain—especially when you decide to go solo. What's often missing from the beautiful images, and the conversation about both opting out and hiking, is the truth about how hard it is. To opt out is to step off the path you're on and start doing what feels right for you. To do it, you have to embrace the fact that it will be an adventure, filled with risks and uncertainty, but also rewards and lessons that could potentially change your life in ways you have never imagined. It's not an easy journey to go on. Personally, the only reason I keep lacing up my boots and doing both is because I know I will never regret trying.

Within these pages, you'll find the mindset and process I have embraced, which you can turn to every time you decide to change paths and hike your own hike in life. As you'll soon see, reaching the first viewpoint can be easy and offers a glimpse of what you're walking toward, and climbing up to the summit for the full view is worth it. But the space between those two peaks is where you will enter a world completely unknown to you, and it is the most difficult part to navigate. To push through, you will need to constantly remind yourself why you're doing this. You don't have to do it perfectly. But you owe it to yourself to at least try. And when things start to feel difficult, you must remember this: *If you want to change your life, you have to change your life.* If you take nothing else from this book, I hope it's that sentence.

I've noticed many people assume that making these decisions must be thrilling, or that you have to be brave to make them. In my experience, and from what I've heard from friends I've met on their own journeys, it's not about either thrill or bravery. If you're on the wrong path, you know it — and you will eventually reach a crossroads where you have to decide whether you're going to stay on it or you're willing to do the work it will take to live differently. I know this journey all too well myself, and will use my most recent opt-out as an example to show you how it looks and feels. I had already opted out of many things before, but deciding to be nomadic for an unknown period of time has been the most confusing one to navigate, because it came — and continues to come — with so many question marks. Throughout my first year, I talked to friends about their own opt-out adventures, and I found so much strength in their words. In this book I have included some of their stories and my favorite pieces of their advice to help illustrate how to work through some of the most critical parts you will face.

It's fair to say that this is more of an emotional guide than a how-to book. It's a look at the human experience you will have when you decide to carve out your own path. I think every person who has opted out of something knows there's no one route that will work for everyone, no one right way to live. They also know that life is a series of adventures. That we live in seasons or chapters. It's not about picking one path and staying on it forever. If you're being really intentional, you will take many different paths in your lifetime. So I can't actually tell you *how* to do this, because our journeys are all so personal—and will continue to evolve, every time we opt out of something new. I also can't tell you if it's going to "work," because I don't know what that word means to you. What I can tell you is this: if you decide to walk into the unknown, no matter what happens next, you will be different on the other side. And when the hard feelings come up? I'm here for you— and so are all my friends in these pages.

It feels important to say here that if you're already happy with the path you're on, you probably don't need to read further. The same goes if you're one of those people who joyfully tackles any physical challenge or seems to skip up mountains. There are so many days when I wish I was one of you, when I wish I wasn't the person who was afraid that nearly every step she took would lead to a fall. Unfortunately, that's not the way I am wired. The process of opting out for me requires a lot of unlearning and becoming, and I wrote this book for anyone else who wants a little support during their own journey.

Finally, I want to add that while this might start off as a solo journey, it shouldn't end that way. I'm not a fan of individualism or living only for oneself, which is what a lot of content in this space can seem to illustrate. From what I've experienced and seen in others, the more you step into who you really are, the more open, compassionate, and generous you can become—and everyone benefits from that.

Adventures in Opting Out, therefore, isn't just another self-help book filled with steps that take you down one particular path. It's a field guide filled with stories about how to lead an intentional life. And while it's not a traditional choose-your-own-adventure book, it *will* help you choose your own adventure. I hope this book leaves you more equipped for your own journey and that you pick it up whenever you feel alone out there.

SECTION 1

The Base

base

Before you take the first step down this new path in your life, we need to talk about what it takes to get to the trailhead at the base of the mountain. The trailhead is the starting point of any walking or hiking trail, and it's the place where your journey physically begins. When it comes to opting out, stepping up to the trailhead is the first day you take action: you quit your current job, buy or list a home, book a flight, decide it's day one of your sobriety, delete a social media account, apply to the school no one thinks you can or should go to, open up your relationship, officially decide not to have kids, walk away from a family tradition, and so on. The act in and of itself is huge. It's the first of all the moments you will experience on this adventure, and the trailhead will forever serve as the juncture where your old and new paths meet. But in my experience, it can take a long time to get here — sometimes even longer than the rest of the hike you're about to go on.

Many of the adventure memoirs I've read have started with the writer being deeply unhappy with some part of their life and making a huge change to shake things up. They do go on adventures, and those adventures teach them lessons and, ultimately, change their lives. But their decisions to go on them are made rather impulsively, and often involve walking away from their lives altogether, and then eventually starting over completely fresh.

Now, I want to make sure I say this: there's nothing wrong with these stories! I've done it a few times myself. And one of my intentions for this book is to deepen our empathy and understanding so we can give our loved ones the space to do what's right for them. So if jumping ship for a period of time is what feels right, and you can do it without hurting yourself or others, go freely, my friend! I will send you off with a hug and a life jacket!

Those memoirs may be the ones that become bestsellers or even get turned into movies because they are filled with ups and downs. It's so much easier to tell (and portray) more climactic stories than it is to show just how long it can take us to make changes in real life. It would be boring to watch an actor complain about the same thing every day for weeks, months, or even years before finally deciding to do something about it. It's also hard to try to portray how it might be to have 90 percent of your life feel pretty good but still know you want something different. So, of course, this is why the majority of our "big life changes" don't get turned into theatrical productions. There aren't enough scenes to keep most people interested in the plot.

Fortunately, there is no pressure for our lives to be so interesting that people would want to play us in a movie. And I truly mean that. It takes a lot of energy to live a dramatic life. Jumping ship and constantly having to try to stay afloat so you don't get lost at sea or ultimately sink sounds like a life of anxiety, instability, exhaustion, and loneliness that I'm just not willing to sign up for. So I'm personally glad and grateful that I can say there is another way.

In my experience with opting out, I have learned that it's perfectly fine to take your time when deciding to change paths in life. Your decision doesn't need to be impulsive. It doesn't have to stem from deep pain. Pain doesn't need to be part of the plot at all! Sometimes you will opt out when everything is fine — even good. Even great! You don't have to run away from your life in order to change it. In fact, it's entirely possible to change one part of your life at the same time you are living the rest of it like business as usual. Instead of jumping ship, you can simply turn a few degrees in another direction and take a single step. Then take another step, and another step, and another—and then look up and around to see if you like where you're heading.

The reason I like taking my time with these decisions is because I tend to believe they are more intentional—which, when eventually acted upon, create longer-lasting change. But in order to make the decision at all, you need to start by figuring out what it feels like to be on the wrong path.

The Wrong Path

I have done plenty of hikes where I've wondered what I got myself into. Or where I've had to give myself countless pep talks to push through. For the latter, I would actually say it happens during a lot of them. But there have been only a handful of hikes where I have cursed and resented nearly every step and considered using all negotiation tactics to get out of it. Where I've wondered what excuse I could come up with to get out of having to climb up or inch down a particularly steep portion. Or where I've suggested we take the easier route the first time and come back to try other routes another day, knowing full well that I will never come back. And if it's a hike I regret agreeing to, I'm usually so anxious beforehand that I wake up and wonder if I can "call in sick." (Since we're being honest, I will admit right now that I have definitely called in sick on a couple of hikes.)

The ones that made me feel so anxious and reluctant? Well, those hikes were usually suggested by other people. That's not to say it was their fault (it wasn't). Remember: in order to go on the hike, I had to agree to their suggestion. So I can't say the words "Sure" or "Yes!" and then point my finger and blame someone else. The problem was that I didn't speak up for myself during the decision-making process. I didn't tell my friends that I was uncomfortable with the terrain, or that I didn't think I was physically capable of completing the hike. I didn't share what I wanted out of the experience, or that I hate doing "busy" hikes where you are surrounded by huge crowds of people. I didn't set my boundary. Instead, I did the exact opposite: I said yes when I should have said no. And then I paid the price and either let my friends down by canceling our plans or laced up my boots and begrudgingly pushed through.

The feeling that I was doing the wrong hike didn't always mean I couldn't actually do it. I think there have been only two hikes where I've had to stop and turn around part of the way through, and those were due to an injury. What made it the wrong hike was that it was simply the wrong choice for me. It wasn't bad, and it wasn't wrong for everyone; it just wasn't right for me. This is the same way I would describe the feeling of being on the wrong path in life. It's not always bad, and it's not the wrong choice for everyone. There are just some paths that haven't felt right for me. These are the ones I've considered walking away from — or opting out of.

If you read my first book, *The Year of Less,* you know that I have a lot of experience with moving. I lived in seven different homes by the time I was eight years old and attended five different schools between first and third grade. At eighteen, I moved out again and have lost count of the number of places — cities and homes — I've lived since.

At the end of that book, I shared that I had made the decision to move back to my hometown in 2015. While I would love to say that was intentional, what I've since realized is that it was actually reactionary. I moved back to Victoria to help my dad, and to attempt to maintain what normalcy looked like for my family after my parents' divorce that year. After writing *The Year of Less,* I finally did some therapy for the first time. In our sessions, I learned that that's how I respond in most dramatic and/or traumatic situations: I step into the role of a rescuer, try to reduce the impact on myself and others, and maintain the status quo. I will never regret moving back to Victoria. It wasn't a bad decision. I reconnected with some of my friends and built deeper bonds with my dad and sister in a way that doesn't always happen when you're an adult. Those are good things. But there were certainly times when I didn't want to be there, and I knew I wanted to live somewhere else in the long term.

Deciding to move to Squamish, where I went next, was then its own adventure in opting out. I was leaving a city of four hundred thousand residents and going to a small mountain town of just twenty thousand that was nearly five hours away from Victoria by both car and ferry. Trading a city where I had a lot of friends for a town where I had zero. I had tested the waters by going on a few extended trips to make sure I really liked it there. And I looked at rental listings and played around with my budget for weeks to make sure the numbers would work. But I was afraid to go. Afraid of what would happen if I wasn't around to maintain the status quo back at home. Afraid I wouldn't make friends. Afraid of the unknown. And really afraid to tell my dad I wanted to leave. Not because he wouldn't understand, but because I didn't want to let him down.

The day I finally recognized that I was in Victoria for the wrong reasons was the day I accepted that it was okay for me to start that conversation with him. That I couldn't keep living my life for other people. Years before, I had all but memorized Bronnie Ware's article listing the top five regrets of the dying, and the first one had always stood out: "I wish I'd had the courage to live a life true to myself, not the life others expected of me." I didn't want to live, let alone die, with that regret. It was a pattern I had repeated for years—at home, at work, in relationships, and so on—and I couldn't keep it up. I knew it would be better for everyone if I was honest about what I really wanted for myself. So I talked to my dad. He fully supported my decision, and even helped me move for the umpteenth time. Nothing fell apart at home after I left. And I went on to spend the next two years creating a beautiful, calm, and creative life in my new town.

Before I later decided to leave Squamish and travel long term, I would never have told you that living there ever felt like the wrong path for me. It wasn't like when I'd moved back to Victoria. I loved Squamish. Seriously: every time I opened the blinds or walked through my favorite part of town, I would look up at the mountains and literally say the words, "I love you, Squamish!" It was the first place I had properly felt at home, and the first place I could ever see myself wanting to save up and buy an actual home in one day. So I wouldn't have said one bad thing about it. But, as time went on, what I *could* have told you was that I wasn't ready to fully settle down yet. I wanted to travel and see more of the world.

As a teenager, I had been jealous of friends who went on family vacations around the world, or who traveled after we graduated. Backpacking around Europe, Australia, New Zealand, and so on. It all looked and sounded incredible. But that wasn't something my family could afford, nor did it seem to be one of my parents' priorities. Together, they retired with a combined sixty-seven-plus years of experience working for the government, and they prioritized benefits (which did help us all) over their interests, and pensions (which I'm grateful that they have) over vacations. To that end, as soon as I was old enough to work, they told me that I had to. And with their practical mindsets and incredible work ethics, they impressed upon me that I couldn't afford to quit a job or take time off in order to travel—which was a luxury, not an acceptable way of living.

I will never resent my parents for teaching me the importance of working hard and being willing to do any job in order to make ends meet. If anything, I have to believe that's part of the reason I am able to live the way I do now—because I've spent years writing during any spare hour I can find and creating a nontraditional career that permits me to work from anywhere in the world. But there is no doubt that their messages also impacted the way I thought I was allowed to live. To that end, it's not surprising that I didn't go on my first solo trip until the age of twenty-eight, when I finally had no debt to my name.

It wasn't a great first trip. I didn't love the city I went to, didn't feel comfortable in the place I stayed, and left feeling certain that I would never go back. And yet, in those four days, I discovered something about myself that I *did* like. On-the-road Cait was more open than at-home Cait. I was curious. Asked more questions. Was willing to try new things. And open to letting things unfold in whatever way they were supposed to. As someone who had grown up with structure and assumed I had to plan my life and goals down to every detail, I found it exhilarating to be so spontaneous. To wake up and let things go with the flow. "Exhilarating" is actually the wrong word to describe it, because the truth is that it felt natural—as if I was completely at ease moving through the day, and the world, in this way. I had just never had the opportunity to do it before. I had never *given* myself the opportunity to do it before.

I continued to experiment with solo travel after that, and my trips varied wildly in terms of length, travel method, destination, and so on. By the age of thirty-two, I had explored many parts of North America, but I still hadn't gotten on a plane and flown overseas. Europe was the one part of the world that I had always felt the most drawn to—the United Kingdom in particular—but I still hadn't gone. I had been told many stories that filled my brain and formed my thoughts about not being able to go there, or why I shouldn't want to go there. Stories about how it was too far, too expensive, too boring, and so on. It all made going feel impossible. But that's what I had always wanted to do. I wanted to go to the UK. I didn't want to leave Squamish forever; I just wanted to go explore this part of the world for a little while. So that's what I finally decided to do. I saved up and booked a trip in the spring of 2018; that's when everything shifted.

It was one of those once-in-a-lifetime vacations. I had made the decision to start saving up for it in August 2017 and got on a plane nine months later, on May 1, 2018. For six weeks, I navigated the trains and visited friends all around the UK, and then hopped over to Ireland and navigated a car on the other side of the road. I walked and hiked constantly, took in classic views of rolling green hills filled with sheep and cows, and got lost in the sheer volume of history the land held. It wasn't all perfect. I moved too quickly, often felt more uprooted than settled, and didn't take good enough care of my mental health. But along the way, I wondered what I could learn from the experience — and if I could attempt to do this again, but move slower and travel for a longer period of time.

By the time I got home to Squamish, something had shifted in me. My friends Azalea and Sian were the first to notice it in the most subtle of actions that only the people closest to you can see. They watched me walk around my condo and sit on the arm of my couch in such a way that they laughed and said, "You don't look comfortable here." I couldn't describe exactly why that was true, but it was. I wasn't comfortable in my own home anymore. I didn't want to be there, and they saw it. I felt it, and they saw it.

The Signs

In order to experience the benefits that could come from going down a new path, you need to understand why you want to step off the one you're currently on to begin with. And in order to do that, you will need to start looking for the signs that you're ready to make a change.

When it comes to deciding which hike to do, you should start by checking in with yourself about how you're feeling and what kind of adventure you want to go on. With that information, you might choose an easier hike because you're either too tired or sore for your usual route. Or you might choose a new hike altogether because you want to challenge yourself or see some new landscapes.

When it comes to opting out, the signs that you're on the wrong path will be determined by whether your current path is leaving you feeling dissatisfied or genuinely unhappy or whether everything is fine and you are still craving something different. Either way, here are just some of the many things you might experience, physically or emotionally.

The Signs

- You complain about the same thing over and over, for weeks, months, or years.
- You feel bored, ambivalent, or even numb about a job, relationship, or situation.
- You have trouble falling asleep.
- You have trouble staying asleep.
- You feel defensive about your choices.
- You feel bad after doing something you've always done before.
- You don't like yourself very much but aren't sure why.
- You don't like thinking about where your money is going/ what it's being used for.
- You feel jealous/resentful when you see other people doing things you want to do.
- You can see the direction you're heading in and you don't like it.
- You feel as though you've settled.
- You feel as though you chose this lifestyle and aren't allowed to change your mind.
- You want things to be simpler.
- You want things to be more interesting.
- You daydream about the past (even the parts that weren't that great but were perhaps simpler or more interesting).
- You daydream about walking away from everything.
- You distract and numb yourself with food/alcohol/shopping/work/screens et cetera.
- You can't stop thinking that there must be another way.

The list goes on and on. Something that fascinates me about this part of the process is that the signs are always right there in front of you. *Always*. I have found no exception to this rule, and it felt especially true after talking to friends for this book. The signs are always big and bold, and can stir up all kinds of feelings and trouble in your life. And the minute you see them, it becomes painfully obvious — to the point where you will probably feel foolish for not seeing them sooner. So how do we miss them?! Why is it so hard for us to see these big and bold signs? From what I've learned and gathered, it's often because we are so plugged into our lives that we end up completely disconnected from ourselves.

By "plugged into," I don't necessarily mean that you are staring into the screens of your phone, computer, or television all day long. You don't have to be living your life online in order to be disconnected from your reality — although that could be true and can be the sign that some people need to see in order to make a change. No, what I mean is a little simpler than that: it's just that we are so busy *living*. Keeping ourselves busy with our routines, going through the motions, doing what we've always done — in all areas of our lives — and believing the stories we've been told, or have even told ourselves, about how and why this is the way it's supposed to be.

In sticking with these routines and stories, we don't give ourselves the time and space to hit Pause, look at our lives objectively, and ask ourselves if it's what we really want. So we miss the signs. We miss the feelings. We miss what our own body and mind are trying to say. We don't notice what's right in front of us, even if it's hurting us or holding us back. And what's worse: we make excuses for it. We invent reasons for why we are staying on the paths leading us to places we don't even want to go.

I say all this with no judgment. I've been in the same situations before I've made most big changes in my own life. Some were more obvious and serious than others. For example, before I stopped drinking for good, I "quit" for forty-five days. Then I went on a two-week bender, when I blacked out almost every night, and put myself in a number of potentially hazardous situations. A few random memories from those two weeks include ditching my friends in the middle of the night during my first trip to New York City, getting into cabs and not knowing where I was going, reconnecting with someone who had hurt me deeply and was truly bad for me, and having unprotected sex. If those weren't big enough warning signs, a smaller one was waking up every morning and seeing that I had deleted my entire phone call and text message history. This was something I regularly did when I was drunk because I didn't want to remember what kind of utter nonsense I had said or done the night before. I didn't want to know who I had hurt, or who might have hurt me. I didn't want to remember and feel any shame. But seeing the empty folders filled me with its own sense of dread.

On a less serious note, the main reason I stopped using certain social media platforms was because I noticed that I always felt negative after being on them. Bad about myself, bad about others, bad about what was happening around the world, and so on. It took a long time, and a lot of experimentation, to ultimately give them up. The story I had been telling myself was that I "needed" the platforms for work. Eventually, though, I realized that my mental health needed to be taken care of *in order* for me to work, and that was a good enough reason to let them go. (Today, I see preserving mental health as the *best* reason to let them go.)

When it came to deciding to give up my home in Squamish

and travel long term, the signs were different still. I could say the idea was planted when I was in the UK that spring, and I couldn't get it out of my head. And let me tell you: if you can't stop thinking about something, that is another sign it's worth considering. I could also say that returning from that trip and feeling slightly uncomfortable in my own home was a sign, and it was. I came back from that trip feeling completely detached from almost everything I owned, and ready to experience a different way of life. Another sign: I noticed that I wasn't excited about making plans that would require me to stay in BC for too long. When friends asked if I wanted to book our usual annual trips or plan some new adventures, I felt suffocated. As if it was a huge commitment, and I would be trapped in a place that was fine but not where I really wanted to be.

I used to describe these signs as gut instincts, as I genuinely believe we know what we need to do, even before we do it. In her book *The Path Made Clear,* Oprah Winfrey calls them whispers, and that feels truer for me now. As human beings, we are born with our own individual level of intuition. But then we are immediately surrounded by people, places, and cultures that influence us—and we stop thinking solely for ourselves. The whispers know how to steer us in the right direction. We just have to start listening.

Options

I talked to close to two dozen friends while I was writing this book, and I asked every single one of them to describe the signs, or whispers, that signaled it was time to opt out of something. Their responses made up much of the list you read in the last chapter, which shows you just how many different feelings and scenarios can prompt people to change paths in life. But two friends shared similar stories with me that I hadn't even considered as possibilities. They didn't see the signs themselves at first. Someone else pointed them out.

When this happens—when someone points out the thing that is so clearly hurting you or holding you back—you can react in one of two ways. You can take it as constructive feedback. Or you can get defensive about why you're doing the thing that's holding you back. My friends shared their experiences with both reactions. I'm going to share Nicole Antoinette's story first, because the experience she was having before someone pointed to her sign was so familiar.

Before we get into that, let me tell you a little more about Nicole. We first connected in January 2017, when she invited me to be a guest on her podcast. At that point, *Real Talk Radio* was already one of my favorites (and continues to be to this day). It's a long-format show where she interviews guests for up to two hours at a time. The topics she has covered since she launched in 2015 are so far-ranging that it's almost impossible to summarize what the show is about. But on the whole, the lengthy interviews create a space for people to dive deep and have refreshingly honest conversations. It is also a space for Nicole to open up about her own life, and to share the ups and downs of her decisions to quit drinking, change her diet, stop running, start long-distance hiking, uncouple from her now ex-husband, and move into a van. In short, she has opted out of *a lot*.

Anyone who has ever listened to the show knows that one of the things Nicole has openly discussed is her long history with insomnia and sleep problems. For a full year, though, she was having a particularly tough time with this and was suffering from the effects. On top of feeling exhausted all the time, she found that she wasn't as mentally sharp, experienced increased anxiety, and overall felt both frayed and limited in what she could do each day. Throughout the year, Nicole tried anything and everything that might help her. She started with the traditional "sleep hygiene" recommendations, including avoiding caffeine, getting some natural light during the day, having an evening routine, creating a pleasant and relaxing sleep space, and so on. She also tried taking over-the-counter sleep aids, such as sleepy tea, melatonin, and other sleeping tabs. At one point, she even tried some stronger sleeping pills but quickly realized she hated how they made her feel.

At most, these "solutions" provided only temporary relief, and sometimes none at all. So, in a last-ditch effort, Nicole decided to see an acupuncturist. After going through an incredibly thorough intake process, in which the acupuncturist learned all about Nicole's lifestyle and habits, she looked at Nicole and asked, *Have you ever thought about taking a break from drinking?*

Now, in case you haven't read my first book, I will explain here that Nicole's and my sobriety stories share some commonalities, the major one being that neither of us identifies as an alcoholic. We weren't addicted to alcohol. And nobody in our lives would've come up to either of us and said they were particularly worried, nor would they have ever encouraged us to quit drinking altogether. (Reminder: If all your friends are on the same path as you, they *won't* suggest that you get off it.) But we *did* have unhealthy relationships with alcohol. And yet because our social lives revolved around it, we just carried on with our drinking habits for years. We stayed on the paths we knew.

The acupuncturist, however, didn't know Nicole. But in getting to know her, she asked Nicole a rather simple question. She didn't ask her to *quit* drinking. She simply gave her a new option, and asked if she'd ever thought about *taking a break* from it. The truth was, Nicole hadn't thought about it. Never. Not once. Why would she? Nobody had suggested it was a problem, nor had they modeled what a sober life could look like. She literally hadn't considered that there might be another way to live. At another point in time, Nicole might have gotten defensive about the acupuncturist's question, but she was exhausted from her lack of sleep. She needed something to change. As soon as someone else suggested an option she hadn't considered, she saw the signs and instantly felt a weight lifted.

You see, while the idea to quit drinking had never been a conscious thought before, as Nicole shifted from her early- to midtwenties, she *did* have a slowly growing sense that she didn't like herself very much. At first she couldn't pinpoint why, but the signs *were* there. The only time she yelled at and fought with her partner at the time was when they were drinking. In terms of her health and safety, the times when she made more reckless decisions were also when she was drinking. And after a night of it, she would often wake up in the morning with a sense of dread. These kinds of low-key discomforts are easy to ignore or mask, which is one of the reasons we can stay on paths for much longer than we should. It's like wearing a dress that's a little bit too tight, as Nicole described it to me. It's not that you can't make it work. And it's not necessarily that most people would even notice. But you would feel so much better if you just changed your clothes— or, in her case, if she just tried removing alcohol from her life.

Nicole didn't know that drinking was impacting her sleep. She wasn't paying attention or seeing the signs. And none of her friends pieced it together either. But then someone else pointed at another path to go down, and the tight dress suddenly seemed a little more obvious. She could let out the breath she didn't even know she was holding while squeezing into it, and try on something in another size. In the end, it was Nicole's *response* to the idea that showed her what the next step was. Her sense of relief at the mere suggestion that there was another way.

Be Safe, Not Sorry

Before I commit to any big decision, I tend to think about everything that could go wrong. I would like to say this reflects the fact that I'm organized and a planner. But the truth is that, for better or worse, this is just how my anxious brain works. Whenever I have an idea, I don't think about what could go right. Instead, I catastrophize it. "What's the worst that could happen?" isn't just a casual question I throw around to inspire myself to stop being scared and start taking risks. No, it is the one big question I ask myself, and then I consider every possible situation in my head, sometimes over and over again.

When it comes to hiking, and especially spending any time in the backcountry, this question can help you plan for things that could physically go wrong. The reality is that you could, in fact, come face-to-face with cougars or grizzly bears. You could also hurt yourself, and be stuck waiting for search and rescue to come and find you (assuming someone in your life actually knows where you are—which we'll get into soon). And avalanches are a very real threat if you venture out into the snow under certain conditions.

When it comes to opting out of things, I can tell you that my level of concern regarding these worst-case scenarios has varied depending on the thing I've given up. Before I deleted my Facebook account, I decided the worst that could happen was that I might lose contact with some friends and/or miss out on some events. Not ideal, but not actually the worst thing that could happen in my life—and something I could take small actions to prevent or remedy. Before I started documenting the shopping ban on my blog, on the other hand, I decided that the worst that could happen was I would fail publicly. This one required a bit more courage and humility but ultimately felt like a risk I was willing to take.

Before I quit drinking, I decided that the worst that could happen was I would lose all my friends and never find a partner who accepted me for who I was. Understandably, this one felt like the biggest risk—and the idea wasn't unwarranted. I've lost only a few friends—people who weren't ready to connect without drinks in our hands. But at the time of this writing, it's been seven years and I still haven't met a man who has been *completely* comfortable with the fact that I don't drink. (Which, yes, I know, means I just haven't been meeting the right people!) Considering that most of my social life, and all of my dating and sex life, previously revolved around drinking, it makes sense that this was my worst-case scenario. Stepping off the path felt like knocking over the first domino in a line. Losing one thing could mean losing it all.

I've opted out enough to tell you that, while it hurts when the worst-case scenario actually happens, it has never been as painful as I'd imagined—especially because, as time goes on, I've always realized that I'm happier on the new path I've chosen. But thinking about what might happen if I gave up my home in Squamish to travel long term came with different considerations than many of my other opt-outs. I had a lot of logistical fears about the travel itself, of course. But the worst-case scenario for me personally was that I wouldn't be able to afford to move back there. Squamish was one of the fastest-growing communities in the entire country at the time, and rents and home prices proved this. When I first moved there, I would look at real estate listings and see one-bedroom condos for between $309,000 and $349,000 Canadian. When I left two years later, starting prices for the same $309,000 units were closer to $425,000. I couldn't afford to buy on my own as it was, but I could still afford to rent there — and if I left and prices continued to go up, there was a very real chance I wouldn't be able to go back.

So, what's the worst that could happen? Even if you don't liken yourself to a planner, if you're leaving for a hike, it's important to know what you could face in the outdoors so you can be prepared. You might pack a bear bell and/or bear spray, take a course in first aid and wilderness preparedness, or save up to buy a proper handheld GPS navigator (versus just relying on your smartphone). You may even decide that you are just not ready for some adventures, and that is perfectly fine too. I will always advocate for being safe first rather than sorry later.

And the same is true for opting out. Knowing beforehand that you could miss out on some events or lose touch with a few friends helps take the sting out of it when it happens. Or knowing that you could make some mistakes helps you *share* those mistakes with anyone you've decided to stay accountable to. And knowing in advance that you could lose aspects of your social life helps you prepare for when you might feel lonely on your new path. It's not just about asking yourself what the worst-case scenario will be. It's about asking yourself if you think you can handle it and not changing paths until the answer is "Yes."

No matter which path you choose, remember that there's always a cost to it. I knew there was a chance I wouldn't be able to afford to move back to Squamish if I left when I did — or at least not without roommates or a partner or some kind of unique living situation. But I couldn't afford to take both paths: to live there *and* travel for extended periods of time. And I wasn't interested in just staying put and living. So, what was the worst-case scenario? Or rather, what price was I willing to pay? Ultimately, I realized that choosing to stay would have been choosing to live with a scarcity mindset. I didn't want to sacrifice something I longed for just because I was too afraid of what might happen after. Even if I couldn't afford to go back to Squamish, I had to trust that there were other places out there for me — and that my journey would lead me to wherever I might enjoy next.

Just Enough Research

I have a love-hate relationship with trail websites. There is a popular one in Vancouver that provides information on hiking trails in the many regions of southwestern BC. I appreciate the basic data points around distance, elevation gain, and the best seasons to complete each hike. But the level of difficulty and estimated completion time is subjective, depending on how much hiking experience and physical capability a person has. And I know that the literal step by step (including pictures) of what the entire thing is going to include can be helpful—but it also runs the risk of taking the *adventure* out of the experience. Or, worse, convincing you that you can't do it before you've ever stepped onto the path.

Having said that, make no mistake: I want you to be smart. It's important to know the expected weather conditions, and to understand what you'll be getting yourself into. But I'm a big advocate of doing *just enough* research—before *any* kind of adventure. I've gone on enough hikes now that I know the three most important things to consider when planning and preparing.

1. I dress appropriately.
2. I know how long I might be out there and I pack enough water and snacks.
3. I understand what kind of terrain it is, what the risks are, and which animals I might cross paths with so I can pack extras like a headlamp, noisemakers, bear spray, knife, rope, et cetera, depending on where I'm going.

Research-wise, I will usually read through the details about a hike one time, but I try not to *study* those details so there is still an element of surprise when I'm on the route. (And I really don't want to know if there are switchbacks because I don't like them; that will almost always convince me not to do a hike!) I also try not to stress about whether or not I can physically complete the journey. If I start the hike and have to stop partway through and turn around, that's okay—but I don't want to make that call before I even begin. I want to get out there and figure out whether I'm capable of doing it or not. And if I'm not, maybe I can learn from that and try it again at a later date, when I feel more equipped.

This concept of doing just enough research—for *anything*—was difficult for me to embrace at first. When I was younger, I was a self-proclaimed and proud planner. My calendar was always filled up weeks in advance, I organized my life down to every possible detail, and I knew exactly what I was striving for—including the feelings I thought I would have. So the idea that I might do just a little research, and then "try and see" how things worked out, was completely foreign to me.

It feels important for me to say that there's nothing inherently wrong with being a planner. I know how much it can help people with busy lives, or even with things like anxiety, to be able to anticipate what's ahead. But something I noticed personally, over time, was that if my daily life or my opt-outs didn't go according to my plan, I often felt disappointed (usually in myself) or even angry (at the situation or at others). These feelings not only detracted from the experience in the moment but often led me to believe it had been a waste of time, which sometimes deterred me from trying again in the future.

When I started playing around with doing only a little bit of research and releasing expectations about how things would go, I slowly discovered the joy of letting things unfold more naturally. It also created space for some spontaneity and surprises to enter the picture. And rather than believing I had full control of a situation and thinking I had to stick to a plan, I began to see everything as a learning opportunity—which taught me so much more about myself, and what I was capable of, than following a specific outlined path ever had.

Now I can't say I've taken this piece of advice before every one of my opt-out adventures. For example, before I quit drinking, I didn't do any research. I just knew I had to remove it from my list of hobbies and decided what the worst-case scenario was. But I didn't know what the specific challenges would be or, therefore, how to prepare for them. Essentially, I just looked to my dad, who had quit drinking when I was a kid, and knew there was another way of living.

But the shopping ban was a great example of doing just enough research before getting started. I essentially looked around my home and wrote a list of rules that made sense based on what I owned and valued. I didn't overthink it. I just looked, wrote, and hit Publish on my blog. In hindsight, I think this is one of the reasons I did the shopping ban at all—

because I didn't give myself time to talk myself out of it. I just started.

If you're thinking of moving to a new city or town, doing just enough research might mean going to visit it a few times or even planning a little staycation there first. That's essentially what I did before moving to Squamish. It's also what my friend Fiona Barrows did before she left London and moved to Frome, in Somerset, England. She booked an Airbnb for one month and explored the town as though she already lived there, and *then* asked herself if it felt like a place she really wanted to move to.

For full-time travel, perhaps the most important thing I had to consider and research was how I would pay for it. The few people I knew who traveled for extended periods of time in their own ways all seemed to handle it differently. My friend Gale Straub (author of *She Explores* and host of the podcast of the same name) and her partner saved what they hoped would be enough money to travel for a year before quitting their jobs, moving into their converted van, and traveling around the United States for about twelve months. My friends Kevin and Mandy Holesh were both self-employed, which made it possible to live and travel around in their camper for many years. And Nicole was self-employed too but had actually opted to move into her van *because* it was more affordable than renting.

At the time I was contemplating my adventure, I couldn't possibly save all the money I would need first because my work was such that I earned very irregular income. (Sometimes I got paid only a few times throughout the year.) So I knew I couldn't save every penny first. But I also knew that, as long as I could stick to my regular monthly budget, I had money coming in all through the year and would be okay. So my budget was the main thing I planned around before giving up my home and getting on a plane. (And finding/buying affordable travel medical insurance too!)

To conduct this "just enough" research, I started by picking a region I wanted to explore. This wasn't hard for me. I hate the heat and therefore have never wanted to go to places like South America or Southeast Asia. I know it's more affordable, but it doesn't feel like a fun option for me. I have, however, always been drawn to Europe. After spending time in the UK, I knew I wanted to see more of it—and move at a much slower pace, to support both my work/routine and my mental health. *What if I picked a few cities there that I could settle into?* I thought. And perhaps I could even live the way many of my European friends lived: they had a home but also traveled a bit, taking advantage of cheap flights and the close proximity of so many amazing cities across the continent.

The downside of wanting to explore the UK—especially on my own—was that it's not exactly cheap. My goal was to attempt to keep my travel costs similar to my costs in Squamish (also not exactly cheap). But thanks to a few websites that help people search for long-term rentals, I found a handful of cities that fit my budget and that I could see myself spending time in. And if my business stayed the same, which it looked as though it would, I'd be able to afford this for at least the next year.

Beyond the budget and cities, I did some quick research around visas. At this time, I learned that as a Canadian I was able to spend six months in the UK as a visitor. Then all I had to do was leave for thirty days before I could go back for another six months. I also learned that I could spend no more than ninety days (in any 180-day period) in the Schengen Area—a zone made up of twenty-six European countries that have agreed not to regulate their borders and to have one common visa that people can use to travel within all the countries. That meant I could leave the UK and pop over to continental Europe for a bit before going back to spend more time there. With that information, I again researched a few more cities that might be both affordable and appealing to me. And that became my plan.

For 2019, I would spend time in just a few cities in the UK and fly over to the continent when I could afford to—or when my six months was up and I needed to leave. I didn't know where I would start yet, or how long I'd be there, or when I'd come home, or what I would do if I changed my mind about any of it. All I knew was that I felt "just enough" ready to go and see what the year could hold for me.

Calculated Risks

Before I switch off this topic of research and preparation entirely, I want to make sure I drive one last point home—as it might be the most important. It's the idea of taking a calculated risk versus being foolish. Out of everyone I interviewed for this book, not a single person shared stories about being reckless. Nobody was impulsive. They all made calculated decisions—weighing the odds against their own level of risk tolerance. And if I had learned anything from writing about personal finance for so many years, it was that everyone's risk tolerance will be different. But these tolerances are all valid and based on an individual's knowledge and experience with a given area.

Some of the opt-out adventures in this book (including my own) will sound like huge leaps into the unknown. Quitting substances, opening up relationships, deciding not to have kids, moving into RVs or to entirely new cities or countries, traveling long term, and so on. You may read some stories and have a few thoughts swirl through your mind along the lines of *I could never do that!* or *What are they thinking?!* These are common trains of thought, especially when it feels counterintuitive for you, or if the example goes way beyond the current boundaries of your comfort zone. But every adventure, no matter how big or small, includes some amount of calculated consideration. These people didn't jump ship. They planned for the worst-case scenarios, did some research, and maybe even experimented with their opt-out for a while first. When the excitement weighed a little more than the fear, they took the first step down their new path.

This is something that I subconsciously knew was true about the opt-out adventures I've gone on myself, but my friend Paul Jarvis helped me see it more clearly. Based on what you might read about him on the internet, Paul seems to be someone who lives 100 percent unapologetically as himself. Over the years, he's opted out of a lot of things: he quit working for an agency to work for himself; he has switched his own business model many times; he was once a touring musician; he moved from Toronto across the country to Vancouver, and then from Vancouver out into the wilderness with his wife; he's vegan; and he doesn't drink anymore either. To an outsider, it might look as though Paul has lived ten lives in his forty-plus years—and to some degree he has. But Paul would be the first person to tell you that doesn't make him a risk-taker. In fact, he doesn't self-define as being risky at all.

While Paul has shared all these aspects of his life (or past lives) in his writing, the thing he is perhaps most well-known for is his philosophy on doing business. He outlines this in his book *Company of One: Why Staying Small Is the Next Big Thing for Business*. Paul's goal with the book wasn't for all readers to go out and start working for themselves—or be literal companies of one person. Instead, he wanted to share his thoughts on why creating a smaller, more sustainable business might be better than constantly focusing on achieving massive growth. And guess what that includes? Making a lot of calculated decisions along the way.

In his own business, Paul sets himself up in such a way that no decision is truly risky. When he left his job at a design agency, Paul set up his own business and started working as a freelance website designer, which was the same work he had been doing at the agency. He then spent the next ten-plus years doing strictly client work, doing business with big brands and building up a reputation for himself, before coming up with the idea for the first digital product that he could sell. It was a vegan cookbook—something he created purely for fun. The goal wasn't to change his entire business model. He just thought, *I want to make this. Maybe people will buy it.*

To his surprise, people did! So he wrote another book, and another book, and each one did better than the last. Then he started creating courses, played around with paid webinars, and started a podcast and got a sponsorship deal for it. A few years later, Paul realized that he was working a fraction of his usual hours and earning a full-time salary from his products, so he decided to stop doing client work. He didn't build a house of cards. He created a solid foundation and then started experimenting with other things. Ultimately, he did walk away from the foundation he had created. But he never would have quit one to try the other. It had to be a calculated risk, and one he felt comfortable taking.

When I started sharing the news that I was going to attempt to travel long term, some people told me I was "brave." One of my friends even assumed that I was "fearless." The truth is that I've never felt like either. I had a very healthy amount of fear. I knew things could (and probably would) go wrong, and that I might be forced to pivot a few times. But I could also counter that fear with a lot of experience. I had spent five years experimenting with solo travel. I liked my own company and liked who I was when I traveled. I also knew what kinds of routines and support systems I needed when I was on the road. Even though I would be physically alone, I knew I couldn't handle being isolated, so it would be important to travel and see friends along the way. And finally, I knew I needed a backup plan—a piece of the puzzle that would make this risk feel a little less foolish and a lot more calculated. For me, that piece was shaped like my dad's house, and it was the last one I needed to complete the puzzle.

Before telling my landlord that I was going to move out, I knew I had to ask my dad an important question: *Could I stay with him for a couple of months each year that I lived this way?* My thought was that I would go home for the holidays and stay for a bit before venturing back out into the world for the rest of the year. In our discussion, we agreed that I would always pay him rent when I was at home. Not quite what I would pay if I lived alone, but a very real amount of money that a grown-up would pay to have a room in a house and to use the water, electricity, and heat within it. Not all the travelers I know do this, but it felt important to us both. I didn't (and still don't) want my decision to "live differently" to come at the cost of anyone else. Thankfully, my dad agreed to this idea—and the very next day I gave my landlord my notice.

Today, I know that I'd be fine if my dad ever said I couldn't stay with him or that he wanted to sell his house. If he did, I could just do the same thing I do when I travel anywhere and find a long-term rental in my hometown. But that was the thing I needed at the time to make my initial decision feel secure, and I'm grateful that he said yes. I also think it's extremely important to acknowledge and share details like this when we talk about how we can afford (financially, mentally, and physically) to take big leaps. Sometimes we can do it on our own, but sometimes there are a lot of other people who help us make it happen. And I can honestly say I wouldn't have done this without my dad's support.

Adventure Partner(s)

As much as I value the experience of completing a solo hike, I will also always tell at least one person where I'm going. If this isn't the number one rule before embarking on any solo outdoor adventure, it should be. Adventures shouldn't be driven solely by your ego. You don't have to prove anything to anyone by secretly disappearing and then coming home and announcing what an epic day you had. Somebody needs to know where you're going and when you expect to return so they can follow up and call for help if they haven't heard from you. It's a simple safety measure. And the fact is that the people you love want you to come home safe and sound (which I assume you want as well!). To help ensure that happens, it would be smart, and kind, to let at least one person know what your plans are.

Depending on the hike, it can also be nice to have someone come along with you. Again, sometimes it's a safety measure—and there really can be safety in numbers. Your partner can also offer an extra set of hands and an additional set of skills. It's actually nice if they have different knowledge and experience, which will prove to be beneficial to you both. You can keep each other company, and give each other pep talks when needed. And you might find that you're able to share the weight, so to speak, as you pack your bags. Whereas individually you would have both had to buy and carry all your own gear, you and your hiking partner might find you can share certain things and, therefore, each pack a little less.

In 2015, my friend Pascal became my official outdoor adventure partner. A few months after I quit my job to work for myself, I realized I wasn't making any time for the things I loved. At the top of that list was spending time with friends in the outdoors. Pascal and I were constantly texting each other about various hikes we wanted to do on Vancouver Island and in and around BC. So one day we decided to create a proper list of hikes and committed to crossing one off the list each week. Because I had the flexibility of being self-employed and Pascal did shift work, we looked at her schedule and found the one day of the week that seemed to always work for us both. That's how Adventure Tuesday was born.

Five years later, I've lost count of how many Adventure Tuesdays we've shared. Not the 250-plus we could have enjoyed if we'd maintained going out once a week for five years—and that's mostly because I moved away and then started traveling more and more. But the exact number doesn't matter. It also doesn't matter that Pascal and I live very different lives. What matters is that, whenever we are in the same city, we always make time to see each other—and we're both happiest when doing that in the outdoors. It's where we can be ourselves and have the most honest conversations. It's also where we are able to support and help each other achieve our goals. Sometimes that means physically holding a hand out and helping the other get to where she wants to go. And sometimes, like when a hike feels impossible, that means reminding each other what we are working toward. That last quality might be the most important one to look for in a person when you want to find a partner for your adventures in opting out.

When you decide to take a new path and live differently from most everyone around you, you will find that a lot of people will encourage you *not* to. They will question your decisions and make you feel as though you're being reckless. Then they will push their own stories or fears on you, and encourage you to stay on the "safer" path. The path that has a clear beginning, middle, and end. The path they've walked and understand. If you pay close attention to the words they say, you'll realize this isn't usually personal. Most people aren't trying to judge or attack your choices. It's really not about you at all. The truth is that most people can see only as far for you as they see for themselves. So the concerns or questions they throw at you are the same ones they would be considering. And if they can't understand why you want to do it, it's only because they can't fathom doing it themselves. It can be hard to remember this in the moment, especially if you're in the middle of it and things feel particularly challenging. But this is why it's so important to find the right person to discuss your opt-outs with. You want the person who will help you *stay* on the new path and do what feels right for *you*.

For the past fifteen years, that person has been my best friend, Emma. If you've read *The Year of Less*, you probably remember her. But in case you haven't, I will just repeat the most important thing I said about her in that book: Emma is the friend who encourages me to make good decisions — the ones that will help me stay on *my* path. She helped me stay positive during my debt repayment journey. She supported me when I quit drinking. She encouraged me when I started taking control of my health, and also when I changed careers, quit to work for myself, did the shopping ban, moved around, traveled more and more—all of it. Emma has never tried to stop me from doing anything I thought was right for me, and whenever I've felt lost or confused, she has always reminded me *why* I'm doing it. She has held space for every idea, every fear, and every possibility because she wants me to be happy and trusts that I know what I'm doing.

As with my relationship with Pascal, it doesn't matter that Emma and I live almost opposite lives. We're obviously not in the same city very often. We also have different backgrounds, as well as different goals and ambitions. But I think that's actually what makes us a great pair. We bring unique knowledge, experiences, and perspectives to the table. And fundamentally, we have the most important thing in common, which is that we love each other and want to help each other grow. I remember being a little scared to tell her I wanted to travel long term, only because I knew the drastic change in time zones would make it more challenging for us to communicate regularly. But deep down, I knew she would support me. Emma was the one person I could rely on to always help me take whatever next step I felt was right for me.

One of the reasons I'm sharing this now is because I hope you can find and choose that person early on in your own adventure. I want you to have at least one person who feels like a safe space, who you can open up to about your fears and concerns, and who can acknowledge and help you work through them without trying to stop you from doing what you want to do. If you aren't sure how to find this person, I would suggest looking at the people in your life and observing which ones are brave enough to do what's right for them. Hint: It's probably the people who are living life a little differently than you. And if you can't think of a single example, it might be time to widen your net and bring some new people into your life.

I'm also sharing this because I hope more of us can become adventure partners for the people we cross paths with in life, and that we can encourage each other, not deter each other, from doing what's right for us. Most of the time when we give advice, we think we are supporting the person who came to us with their problems. But the reality is that sometimes that support feels more like the crushing of one's dreams. And it's really not up to us to decide what anyone else's dreams are, or to control how they live their lives.

So, who would you rather be? The person who tries to convince someone not to go after what they want, simply because you would be afraid to do what they are thinking about doing? Or the person who holds out their hand and helps people get wherever they want to go?

Experiment

There's a quote floating around that never seems to be linked to anyone that says, "Life is a collection of adventures." If I'm really honest, I mostly saw it used in dating app profiles before I opted out of using them. You would think the quote might have piqued my interest, but really I just wondered where all these men got the idea to use the same quote. *Is it from a movie? Or in an article that lists the top ten tactics to get more matches?* I'm digressing here. What really interests me about this quote, and why I think it catches my eye every time I see it, is that it's the exact opposite of the way I was raised to think. Life was supposed to be a collection of steady employment and assets, wasn't it? Of working hard, saving your money, buying a home, maybe getting married and having kids, and then retiring and traveling after that. There was a path to go down, and it was very clearly marked by my parents and many of the friends around me. Adventures weren't on it, nor were they encouraged to be taken.

After my first twenty-seven years of life, though, I reached a juncture with a new trailhead. Its two arrows pointed in opposite directions: one down the path where I could continue working for the government, and the other toward a career in the private sector. A few months later, I reached another juncture with two paths, one leading to a life with alcohol and one to a life without. These junctures have continued to pop up for me every few months or years. And if I'm not paying attention, I miss them — at least until the signs are bigger and bolder or truly in my face. When I finally see them and start to think about changing paths, I do a little research and plan for my personal worst-case scenario. I might also run it by Emma. But ultimately, the most important question I ask myself is if it's worth *trying*.

The word "trying" itself is so freeing. Like there's no perfect path or goal. You can just try something new and see what happens! As you would with a science experiment, you could collect some data on yourself! It's funny, then, how freedom can also be scary. That not knowing what you're walking toward can make it feel impossible to know which steps to take. And it's especially difficult to explain to others what you're doing when you don't know what the exact goal is or why it's one you might want to achieve. So for all these reasons and more, it's completely natural to be afraid of entering the unknown. This is why embracing your opt-outs with an adventurous mindset is so important. If you're curious about how to start, I would suggest turning each opt-out into an experiment.

When Nicole's acupuncturist asked if she'd ever thought about taking a break from drinking, her honest answer was no. At that point, so much of her identity was wrapped up in being a party girl that she couldn't imagine what her life would be like without alcohol. She also couldn't imagine what her friends or partner would think or say. But the idea gave her such a strange sense of relief that she got curious and decided to ask more questions. When her acupuncturist suggested she give up alcohol for just five weeks to see if it helped with her insomnia, that felt doable. It wasn't a full lifestyle change. It was simply an experiment.

These kinds of timelines, or markers, have been used by many of the friends I interviewed for this book. Gale and her partner planned to live in the van and travel for up to one year. Most of the changes Paul has made in his business came after experimenting and ultimately reaching certain financial milestones. Fiona's move to Frome and the moves and travels undertaken by other friends were all a little more open-ended, but they went knowing they would stay for as long as it felt like the right place for them. Not many people started down a new path with the assumption that they could never turn around or change directions again. Instead, they gave themselves the freedom to change their minds if they didn't like where the new path was taking them.

Of course, it's worth mentioning here that there are a few opt-outs you might not be able to go back on. Deciding not to have your own child/children is one that comes to mind. For most of my life, I had assumed I would have them. It wasn't until I was thirty or so that I realized having kids and becoming a parent was a choice. The summer I turned thirty-four, I was finally clear on the fact that it didn't feel like something I wanted to do. I can't exactly turn this opt-out into an experiment. But every year, what I can do is check in and ask myself a few questions: *Did you think about wanting kids this past year? Do you ever feel jealous of people who have them? Does it still feel like something you don't want to do?* While there will come a point when I can't have my own kids, I can still ask myself these questions for years to come. As long as I'm being honest with myself every time, I will make the right decision for me on this—and any other adventure in opting out.

Over the years, people have asked how I have found the willpower to change so many things about my life. I don't believe willpower has much to do with it. I've simply embraced adventure as a mindset, which allows me to accept that any difficulty I face is a challenge I can overcome, not a roadblock for life—even if that means I change paths again or have to turn around. This brings me back to the question I asked myself before I committed to the idea of long-term travel: *What if it doesn't work?* It was a question I'd asked before every single one of my opt-out adventures. This time, I finally knew I would never be able to answer it. You can't know what's going to happen or how you're going to feel about it until you start going down the new path. Instead, you have to work past the fear of doing it "wrong" or "failing" and simply *try*.

Remember that to opt out is to step off the path you're on and start doing what feels right for you. To do it, you have to embrace the fact that it will be an adventure filled with risks and uncertainty, but also rewards and lessons that could potentially change your life in ways you have never imagined. If you look at it like an experiment, it becomes an opportunity to gain new experience and learn along the way. Before I quit my job to work for myself, I told myself that even if it lasted for only six months, it would be worth it. And before I left Squamish, I told myself that even if I only got to travel for 2019, it would be worth it. I didn't need to know what would happen after. I knew only that 2019 was going to be a year filled with adventures. It would be worth *trying*.

SECTION 2

The Viewpoint

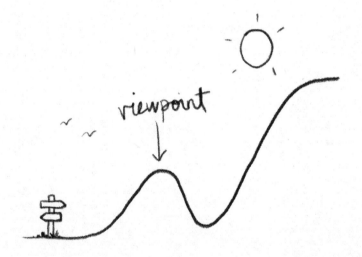

My favorite part of a hike is often the first fifteen minutes of it. That probably sounds slightly discouraging, considering that most of the hikes I do are between one and five hours long. So I will preface this entire section—and really, the rest of this book—by saying that there are lots of other delightful moments throughout the journey. If there weren't, I would never bother to complete one! It just so happens that the first fifteen minutes often ends up being my favorite memory.

Something magical happens when you take the first few steps down a new path you've never explored before. It's like entering a world you didn't know existed, made up of a combination of terrain you've never set foot on and landscapes you've never seen. New territory, therefore, requires you to use all your senses because you can't get by on muscle memory when you're exploring it. Every step demands that you look down, and then up and all around, so you know where you're going and what you must do in order to get there. *Do you need to watch out for tree roots or rocks? Try not to slip in mud? Understand the depth of the carved-out stairs? And are you wearing the right footwear?*

Once you're a little more comfortable with the physical challenge, you can then start to appreciate the sights and sounds around you. Like how the sunlight sparkles like a disco ball as you walk through the trees, or how it beautifully backlights plants and flowers on an open path. Or how the sound of water trickling near the base of a mountain fills you with excitement at the idea that you might find a waterfall the farther up you go. And the animals! There is nothing quite like seeing a new animal for the first time, and when you're in its natural habitat no less. I've still never seen a moose (which makes me sad and think they should probably take away my Canadian passport). But the first time I saw an elk in Squamish, the sheer size of it took my breath away. Spotting an adorable little chipmunk for the first time, on the first peak of the Stawamus Chief, caused the same reaction. Even if you've seen and heard similar things before, no two hikes are exactly the same, so it all comes as a surprise.

The element of surprise is also what makes the beginning of opting out feel as though you're on the right track. Like when you decide to change your diet and notice how many options actually *are* available at your favorite restaurants and stores, which suddenly makes it feel all the more doable. Or when you've been logged off of social media for a few days and start to recognize how good it feels to be present with the people you spend time with in real life. Or when you decide to move to a new city or town and you find a park or coffee shop or grocery store that you know you're going to love. It doesn't always happen in *literally* the first fifteen minutes, of course, but keep your eyes and ears open in those early days. When you decide to take a new path and are truly open to where it could lead you, I find there are lots of little moments of awe and wonder in the beginning. It feeds your confidence and makes you all the more excited to see what's around the next bend. And if you don't stop to enjoy these moments, who will?

The better question, though, might be, what should you do *after* you've taken those first few steps? Because shortly after you start your adventure, you *will* begin to see signs that you're on the right path. Eventually, you will even get to a place that offers the first sight of what you're working toward. If you were on a hike, I would call this the moment you've reached the first viewpoint. It can be the most motivating part of the journey, and sometimes it feels as though it was almost too easy to get there. Why wouldn't you keep going? But eventually, you will *also* get to a place where the path seems a little less exciting and looks a lot more like work. And in my experience with both hiking and opting out, this is where you will have to decide if it's worth continuing down the new path or not. I hope this section helps you navigate the ups and downs of the early days of your adventure. If you can learn how to enjoy and work through them, you'll be better set up for the rest of your opt-out experience.

Start Slow

In my early hiking experiences, I had a really bad habit of trying to keep up with my friends. I don't know if you can call it a "bad habit," per se. I know it's only natural to want to have company, and that it hurts to be left behind. But in trying to move at their pace, I wasn't speaking up for myself or asking for what I needed. This meant I was ignoring various pains. Pretending that my ankle wasn't rubbing against the back of my boot, or that my injured hip wasn't flaring up. It also meant I was panting harder than was probably healthy, and feeling sick to my stomach at times. All because I didn't want anyone to think I couldn't do what they were doing, or didn't want to, worse yet, be left behind.

This is, unfortunately, altogether too common — and the sentiment could be applied to many situations in life. Most injuries occur in the beginning stage of a hike, the same way many of us can burn out at the start of a big adventure in opting out. We've either bitten off more than we can chew or decided to move at a pace that's too quick for us — or both. Or we're too afraid to change our minds or simply change a few rules (that are self-imposed, I might remind you!). Whatever the reason, it keeps us on a path we don't necessarily want to be going down, at a pace we aren't comfortable moving, and it always leads to trouble.

In trying to keep up with others on a hike, there were many times when ignoring symptoms ended with me getting hurt. Taking off my boot to find a massive blood blister — the worst of which were ones that had already popped. Realizing that my aching hip was actually going to leave me with a limp for the next week. Getting a stress fracture that required me to keep my foot elevated for six weeks was probably the most annoying injury of them all. These were all painful and entirely preventable. Suffering through the pain also meant I wasn't enjoying any part of the hike and was relieved when it was over.

When you're trying to keep up with other people who are also opting out, the results are usually a little less physically painful but equally frustrating. Ignoring the whispers that are trying to tell you to trust yourself to do what's right for you. Beating yourself up over the fact that you can't seem to follow the rules that worked so well for others. Wondering what's wrong with you. And, the worst result of all, giving up and then telling yourself you are a failure.

Thinking back on all the solo travel I've done, I can now see that I often started at a pace that was unsustainable. For my earliest trips, I would write a long list of things I wanted to see, and then spend entire days running around and coming back each night in physical pain — all so I could cross as many things off the list as possible. I saw a lot of things, but I didn't really remember them or absorb any detail. I could tell you what I did, but I couldn't tell you about all the interesting people and places I walked past in order to do those things. I was in a rush, so I missed it. Over time, I learned my lesson and started to write shorter lists. Eventually, it got to a point where I would write down only one or two things I wanted to do while I was at my destination. Everything else would be a surprise.

For a reason still unbeknownst to me, during my first trip to the UK, in 2018, I threw all this experience and knowledge out the window. Instead, I traveled around constantly, staying in a place for typically no more than two nights before moving on to the next. I had friends to see, and hikes to do, and libraries and bookshops to visit. And the more people I talked to, the more I added to my list. I got to see and do almost everything—but I suffered. I thought I was having fun. For the first four weeks, I would have told you I was enjoying myself. But after I made my way up to Edinburgh—where I was going to spend four full days—I finally had enough time to settle in and recognize that my mental health was not okay. This realization came on a solo hike, of all places. I knew something was wrong before I even started. Then I choked back tears all the way up Arthur's Seat, sat down at the summit, and broke into a full sob. I sat on the top of an extinct volcano, looking over a city (with a castle sitting on top of another extinct volcano, no less!) that everyone had told me I would love, and cried for more than two hours.

Edinburgh then became the first city that I listened to my body in. The city in which I walked around aimlessly and stopped to look at anything that caught my eye. The city in which I came back to my flat early, cooked myself a healthy dinner, had a hot bath, and read a book before bed. The city in which I stopped worrying about missing out on all the things everyone else told me to do and see and started prioritizing my own needs. Things didn't magically get better in Edinburgh. I still had two more weeks of fast-paced travel to get through, all of which had been booked and paid for. But I learned a tough lesson on that trip: I couldn't travel that quickly in the future. It was a mistake I wasn't willing to make again.

When thinking about what 2019's adventures could look like, I knew I had to move slowly. I had heard about "slow travel" from a few friends—the idea that you don't create an itinerary or rush around, but instead slow down and enjoy a city or town the way a local might. The intention behind it is both personal and more sustainable—a different experience for you, and one that hopefully has less impact on the places you visit. It also gives you the opportunity to see how other people live, and perhaps even learn how to live as though you're a local yourself. This is what I wanted. So I decided that I would stay in places for a minimum of one month at a time. And the cities and towns I went to would be chosen by me, not at the suggestion of others.

The painful results of trying to keep pace with others in the outdoors are physical and, so long as they aren't too serious, can hopefully be remedied with a combination of rest and physiotherapy. But the results of trying to keep pace with other opt-out adventurers? Well, that damage is a little more psychological. It leaves you in a constant comparison trap where you will forever feel as though you're not good enough. And why? Just because you didn't change your life in the exact same way someone else did? Or because you've set rules for yourself that are too strict or even impossible to stick to? I sat on the top of Arthur's Seat for two hours that day in 2018 and wondered what was wrong with me that I couldn't travel the way other people did. Why couldn't I just be happy and beam with gratitude at every stop I made? Why was I crying? The answer was hard to learn but simple enough to understand: because I'm not all other travelers.

This is one of my biggest problems with the self-help space in general: the idea that is sold to us is that if one person can do something, anyone can do that same thing. How many times have you read those exact words in a book or Instagram post? "If I can do it, you can do it too!" Instead, what we should be saying is that if one person can change their life, it's just proof that it's possible for a person to change their life. That's it! It doesn't actually matter what exact steps they took to make it happen, because those exact same steps will not work for everyone who reads them. The only thing you should take from their experience is inspiration that it's possible to change your life too.

One of the main points of this book is to showcase that there are multiple paths we can take in life. No two paths are the same, just as no two people are the same. And even if two similar people tried to walk down the same path, they would still see it differently, because we all bring different knowledge, experiences, and perspectives to every situation we find ourselves in. With this in mind, please, please, please: give yourself the permission and the grace to move at your own pace, right from the start. This is *your* adventure. Nobody else's. Not your parents' or your friends' or your partner's or your coworkers' or that of the adventurers you look up to. It's all yours. So don't try to keep up with other people. Instead, set your own goals and move at your own pace until you figure out what feels natural for you. Even if you don't "see and do" everything, you will at least be a little more comfortable — and might actually enjoy the journey.

Good Enough

On the topic of going slow, there is really no better person for me to introduce you to than my friend Brooke McAlary. Brooke is the host of a podcast called *The Slow Home*. She has also written a book called *Slow*, as well as a previous one called *Destination Simple*. To say that she knows a thing or two about this topic is an understatement, and that's because of all the work Brooke has done to slow her own life down. And her story is one I hold close to my heart and think of whenever I feel as though I'm going even slightly off track with my own goals and values.

In 2011, Brooke's life probably would have looked ideal from the outside. She was married; ran her own jewelry-making business from her home in Sydney, Australia; and had one child and another on the way. What an outsider couldn't see was that Brooke's husband, Ben, was working so much that he was rarely home during daylight hours. She also wouldn't have admitted it then, but Brooke didn't like making jewelry. Honestly, she didn't even like wearing jewelry. She had started the business with only one goal: to be able to work from home. She had gotten so busy that she had to produce more than two hundred pieces per week, and she hated everything about it. The work. The time. The commitment. It didn't help that—unbeknownst to her—she had also been quietly suffering from postpartum depression since she'd given birth to her first child.

Shortly after their second child was born, Brooke found herself in her darkest moment: looking into a mirror, repeating the words "I hate you, I hate you, I hate you," and wondering if her family would be better off if she wasn't there. Fortunately, she recognized that this wasn't who or how she wanted to be, and she told Ben that she wasn't well. They took immediate action to find her help, via doctors, antidepressants, and a therapist. And just as Nicole's acupuncturist was the person to prompt her first opt-out adventure, Brooke's new therapist prompted hers as well. After learning about Brooke's lifestyle and obligations, her therapist asked a simple enough question: *Have you ever considered slowing down and doing a little bit less?* And Brooke's initial response, just like Nicole's, was a flat-out no.

Beyond the no, though, Brooke felt defensive about her choices and was genuinely annoyed by the suggestion that she make different ones—and she wasn't afraid to tell her therapist so. "No one I know does that!" she threw back at her. "That would make me boring, or average, or mediocre, or lazy." And in Brooke's opinion back then, more than anything else, you were not allowed to be lazy. Knowing better than to argue with a patient about the stories they tell themselves, her therapist left the idea in Brooke's hands, which she later took to her computer. She typed her own simple enough question into a search engine: "How do I simplify my life?" That's when she found a website called Zen Habits, and the first article at the top was about decluttering.

The website's creator, Leo Babauta, wrote about a number of other ways people could change their habits or try to simplify their lives, but they all felt too overwhelming for Brooke. Exercise? She couldn't even get out of bed some days. Meditate? She does it now, but her initial thought back then was, *Please, no!* Yet the topic of decluttering kept coming up, and each time it did, it felt easier and easier to digest. Was it possible for Brooke to get rid of some of the vast amounts of stuff in her house? And would that help at all? She didn't know what the process was supposed to look like, or where it would ultimately lead her. But she talked to Ben, who told her to go for it, and she started by setting a timer for fifteen minutes.

It didn't matter what she accomplished in those fifteen minutes. Brooke's only goal was to take action. To spend fifteen minutes each day doing something that would help her with these new decluttering efforts. And when the timer went off, she not only allowed herself to stop but also granted herself the freedom to say that whatever she had done was *good enough.* That concept—to do just enough of something—was far outside Brooke's comfort zone, but it was the rule she needed in order to even get started. It was interesting, then, for her to quickly recognize the link between action and her mental health. Energy seemed to beget more energy because after the timer went off, she almost always thought, *I want to do more.* Sometimes that meant more decluttering. But sometimes Brooke channeled that extra energy into going for walks, or doing a bit of gardening, or playing with the kids. It didn't have to be perfect. She simply allowed herself to do what she could with the time and energy she had.

Slowly, over the next two years, Brooke went on to declutter more than twenty-five thousand items from her home. Brooke also gave up her jewelry-making business and eventually started her podcast. And in the years since, she and Ben continued to downsize, to the point that they even sold their home and ended up traveling around North America with their two kids for sixteen months. This whole life-changing journey wasn't always easy, and there were certainly times when they worried what people would think. Even if we don't like admitting it, it's hard to completely strip ourselves from wanting to feel the acceptance that comes from fitting in, or the validation from others that we are doing the right thing. But by slowing down and doing a little bit less, Brooke and Ben have been able to carve out a path that's right for their family—and there's nothing more meaningful than that.

What I love most about Brooke's story is that she didn't start with a big goal in mind. She also had no idea that she would ever become a trusted podcaster and author on this subject. That wasn't her intention. All Brooke wanted was to get some of her life back—and to come back to herself—and she did a good enough job of that, fifteen minutes at a time.

Your Seventh Sense

As humans, we have the pleasure of being able to take in the world with any combination of the five senses we may have. There's also a lot of talk (and even a movie) about a sixth sense. Some people consider it a sense of danger, but I think it's more like intuition—a feeling that something is happening, or going to happen soon, that can't yet be identified. Before I left Squamish, I started going for regular walks with a new friend, and I noticed she seemed to be equipped with a *seventh* sense—a way of seeing the world around her that I hadn't witnessed before. I like to think of it as a sense of wonder.

From the moment we stepped onto a path, Alanna would start to take in every little thing that caught her eye—things I probably never would've noticed. Like the tiny fuzzy caterpillar that was crawling alongside us, or the slug that was camouflaged by the dirt around our feet. To most people, including myself at the time, these weren't important details. They were just part of the ecosystem. But to Alanna, these weren't just details—they were important characters in the story of this particular walk of ours. So she would point them out, announce her excitement, and then give them a warm welcome and bring them into the narrative. *Who were these little creatures? Where did they come from and where were they trying to go?*

Aside from admiring the creatures we cross paths with, Alanna's curiosity and value for learning cause her to constantly hit Pause and ask questions about everything she sees on her journey. So she will stop to take pictures of trees she can't identify or berries she isn't sure are edible, and then go home and research until she finds the answers. (Then she texts the answers to me, to make sure I'm learning too!) And before carrying on down the path, Alanna smiles — the happiest, friendliest smile you can imagine a person mustering up — and takes the deepest breath. The kind of breath where you can feel the air move through your nose, fill up your lungs, puff out your chest, and give you the oxygen you need to take your next steps.

Alanna isn't just happy to be out on a walk. She treats each one as if it's an adventure, and she takes it all in with a sense of wonder — even if it's a walk we've done dozens of times before. She's filled with a level of awe that allows her to constantly expand her awareness and imagination for what's possible in this little corner of our world. I'd never met anyone like her before, and I still don't think I've met anyone who can match this ability of hers. It was noticeable to me right from the start because for most of my own life, I had walked through this world feeling as though I needed to have all the answers and couldn't possibly admit when I didn't know something. So who was this person who *marveled* over what she didn't know? Who made up stories about what was possible? How did she do this? And if I couldn't pack her in my bag, how could I bring Alanna's seventh sense with me to the UK?

The way I planned to travel in 2019 would involve setting up a home base in a new city and staying there for at least one month at a time. The goal, of course, was to create a routine that would support both my work and my mental health. But I also wanted to enjoy this new part of the world. To not just live the way a local would, but to actually walk around and see what makes it special. After I booked my flight to the UK, I decided to start by giving myself four days off to properly relax and enjoy this new life I was creating for myself. A place to land and deal with jet lag, but also to wander and think about what might be possible. A little vacation before the real adventure began.

I landed at Gatwick Airport on the morning of March 28, 2019 — a date that was right before one of the many Brexit deadlines, and that I had intentionally chosen just in case it actually happened and there were travel disruptions. From there, I rode the train for forty minutes down to Brighton and checked into an Airbnb. And after sleeping for nearly sixteen hours, I woke up on the morning of March 29, got dressed, and walked out into the city with Alanna's seventh sense in my pocket.

To paint a picture of my first destination, Brighton is the largest and most popular seaside town in the UK, partially because of its location (just forty-seven miles south of London — a quick train ride away) and partially because of what it's known for. Dubbed the happiest place to live in the UK by some and the hippest by others, Brighton is a fairly progressive city. There's a huge arts and music scene, and it is unofficially known as the gay capital of the UK. For all these reasons, I can see why some people love it and would choose to live there. Personally, Brighton is a bit too touristy for me.

As the top destination for "hen dos" and "stag dos" (bachelor-ette and bachelor parties), it has too many people—and certainly too many people doing the one thing I never do now (drink). But I hadn't chosen this city for any of those reasons. I decided to start my trip in Brighton because it had been so hot the last time I was there that I couldn't enjoy it the way I wanted to. Essentially, it was a do-over.

For the next three days, in perfect spring weather—59 degrees Fahrenheit (15 degrees Celsius)—I walked up and down the streets and stopped to look at anything that caught my eye. Beautiful book covers in huge window displays. Black spiral staircases that contrasted with the light-colored homes they went up behind. Narrow alleyways covered in graffiti in the North Laine. Signs outside stores, like THE IMPLICATIONS OF CLIMATE CHANGE CALL FOR CONSUMER CHANGE outside the FAIR shop. And what remains of the West Pier out in the sea. I also asked every owner if I could pet their dog, and I talked to every dog as if they were an old friend. I listened to the tide wash up onto the pebble beach. It sounded exactly the same as it would have back home, but the red rocks were alien to my Pacific Northwest eyes. And at night, I looked down the street and saw the sea from my flat and marveled at the way the sun hit the row of homes across from mine and turned their muted yellow paint into a bright gold.

Even though I was there for only four days, I lived like a local while I was in Brighton. I would go to a coffee shop in the mornings, walk around neighborhoods during the day, and come home, cook dinner, read, and relax at night. One day, Kate even came down from York and we attended an author event put on by Matt Haig, who was promoting his book *Notes on a Nervous Planet*. This was my life, just in a new city.

On my last full day in Brighton, I met up with my friend Meg, and together we took the train out to Seaford and walked along the Seven Sisters — a famous series of chalk-white cliffs along the English Channel. We stopped constantly and took in the views from every possible angle. I noticed more and more details as we went, asked questions, and was grateful that Meg (like many Brits) seemed to be filled with knowledge and fun facts. I realized that I barely knew anything about this country I was in, but suddenly I wanted to know everything. And I didn't know how long I would be in the UK, but it already felt like not enough time. Thirteen miles later, I smiled and took a deep breath. The kind of breath where you can feel the air move through your nose, fill up your lungs, puff out your chest, and give you the oxygen you need to take your next steps. I had discovered my seventh sense along the Seven Sisters, and I would try to take it with me everywhere I went.

Say Yes

There are a lot of books and articles out there (and really just a whole lot of Instagram posts and memes on the internet) telling us to start saying no more often. No to plans. No to extra commitments. No to anyone or anything that will use up any of our precious time or energy. And I get why these prompts exist. Heck, in a way, you could even say that this book is one of them. *Say no to living life on someone else's terms!* So I won't sit here and say that the idea of using the word "no" more often is necessarily wrong or even misguided. But what I will say is that there's not enough dialogue about *why* we should be using this word. Memes will never paint a full picture. It's not about shutting ourselves off from the world, which is what most of these images might have you believe. When it comes to opting out, it's about creating space so there's room for more of what brings you joy and of what you find valuable to enter your life—and that includes new people.

When I booked my trip to Brighton, I had intended to spend most of my time there alone, aside from seeing Kate and Meg. But on my first full day there, I got a message on

Instagram from an old blogging friend. Chris Enns was one of my favorite Canadian personal finance bloggers. We had communicated online for years but met only once before—at a conference in Toronto, and for all of five minutes. In fact, it was basically just enough time for both of us to say, "Hi, I love everything you do!," and give each other a big hug. That was in the fall of 2014. We had spoken online only a bit since then. So to get a message from Chris in March 2019 was such a nice surprise—mostly because I was not at all prepared for what it said.

Chris had watched the Instagram stories of my solo wander around the city, and he explained that his wife, Mimi, had an opera performance contract in the UK for four months. They were due to arrive the next day, and he was curious if I really was in Brighton, because they had also decided to "land" and relax there for a few days to start. The only appropriate way to respond to this news was with a very excited *DO YOU WANT TO MEET FOR COFFEE ON MONDAY MORNING?!* Thankfully, he responded with an equally excited *YES!*

After dealing with the usual confusion that can occur when two foreigners try to find each other in a new city, Chris and I met shortly after ten on my last morning in Brighton. For the next two hours, we rambled between topics in a way that people who have previously only really crossed paths online can. We knew so much about each other and yet nothing at all. We knew so many of the same people (because the Canadian personal finance space is teeny tiny, not unlike our overall population), and yet we had very different relationships with them. And we had so many of the same topics on our minds: traveling long term, not knowing when and where to eventually settle, and how to be okay with the fact that it's perfectly okay not to have any answers. Chris and Mimi had left Toronto in November 2018 as well, and they were traveling to wherever Mimi's contracts took them. They did still have a home that they were subleasing out, but they didn't know how long they would be living and traveling this way. They also didn't know if Toronto was the place they wanted to return to.

If anyone had been listening to us, they would have heard two people bouncing around from topic to topic, seemingly without reaching any conclusions, because that's exactly what we were doing. And I can say that switching subjects partway through and moving on to the next wasn't particularly comfortable at times. Our minds want answers. We want to feel as though we are working toward something. We want to know where the path is leading and where we will end up. But by the end of our first coffee, Chris and I agreed that this would be the only rule for our conversations going forward: to never pressure each other to have answers or leave with takeaways. The ramble was good enough.

The only "plan" we made at the end was that we would, in fact, do this again. In this first ramble of ours, we had discovered we would all be in London for the month of April. I was taking the train up that afternoon, so I told Chris to send me his address after he arrived and got settled in. A few days later, I was hanging out at my friend Saima's flat, where I was staying, when his text message came through — and I nearly stopped breathing. Chris and Mimi's address was just seven digits off from Saima's. Directly across the street. I looked outside and sent Chris a picture of his building. (Then I laughed and admitted I felt like a stalker.) He invited me over, and twenty minutes later, we were drinking coffee and laughing about the impossibility of it all in his new living room. In a city with thirty-plus boroughs and more than nine million people, the odds of two old Canadian personal finance blogging friends not only finding themselves in London at the same time but also finding themselves neighbors were not good. We would never be able to understand how that happened. But we didn't need to know how or why. We didn't need the answers. The only thing that mattered was that when the opportunity to spend time together presented itself, we said yes.

I know that other opt-out adventurers won't be able to replicate the story of Chris and me finding each other in the UK. I know this because the odds were seemingly impossible for us. But what can be replicated is my initial approach to the adventure. Like Alanna in the outdoors, I went into this trip with my eyes wide open, and sure enough, I found some magic — and a new friend — right at the start. A character who I didn't know would enter the plot, but who understood me and quickly made me feel as though I was on the right path. While your character might not be named Chris, if you open yourself up to new experiences, you will find people who understand why you've chosen this new path for yourself. Of course, I hope they arrive early and can keep you company or at least provide some support along the way. But more than anything else, I hope you at least see them and acknowledge their presence.

Hi, Friend

With more and more people spending time outdoors as well as changing paths in life, this feels like a great time to address the topic of trail etiquette. Etiquette, in general, is a set of rules that are considered to be polite behavior in any situation. In the outdoors, there are a few essentials to keep in mind. Near the top of the list, you should always pack out what you pack in, which translates: take your trash home with you! If you're on a mixed-use trail where you might cross paths with mountain bikers or people riding horses, you should look for the signs that outline who yields to whom. (Personally, I think that as a hiker it's usually just easier for me to move out of the way for anyone!) And if you're planning to use your phone, do everyone a favor and either wear headphones or keep it on Silent mode. Nobody wants to listen to your music, audiobook, or podcast of choice, and they definitely don't want to hear the buzz that sounds every single time you get a text message.

What you don't always see is that there is one unspoken piece of etiquette that isn't usually listed on these signs but is just a nice thing to do, and that's smiling and greeting everyone you cross paths with. Sometimes this is a simple act of courtesy. If you're about to pass someone, especially at a quicker speed than they are moving, it's kind to announce yourself first—mostly so they aren't alarmed by your sudden appearance. You can say things like "Hello up there!" or "Passing on your left!" Or if you're coming down from the summit and passing people who are hiking up, a simple "You're doing great!" or "The view is so worth it!" can offer some much-needed encouragement.

Beyond the courtesy and encouragement, though, greeting people could also be an extra measure of safety. What if you got hurt out there or went missing? I know this is one of those worst-case scenarios, but it happens more than we'd like to believe. If your face was flashing across the news, someone might be able to identify where they last saw you. Swap places and think about the fact that you might be able to identify them if the tables were turned. How much more important does it feel to say "Hello" now?

Simple greetings feel even more important to me when I consider it from the perspective of how it feels to be opting out and taking a new path in life—which is why I would disregard those vague memes about saying no and putting such high boundaries around yourself that you completely close yourself off. Because *hello,* you are already alone out there! You don't need to isolate yourself further. In fact, I would really recommend that you don't. I know it's not always easy to announce your presence, or even to offer encouragement to others, when you feel as though you have no idea what you're doing yourself. (I say this as someone who is fairly introverted, isn't comfortable in group dynamics, and for a long time suffered from a serious lack of understanding regarding why anyone would want to be my friend.) But if we walk around just saying no to everything that doesn't perfectly align with an idea we have about ourselves or our lives, it strips us of the opportunities to find people who might be on similar paths. Or the chance to lend a hand and help someone else.

What I've come to believe about this topic is that the no — or the silence—protects only you. Your boundaries, your time, your energy. And there are times in life when you will absolutely need to protect yourself. For example, when I'm working on a deadline, I basically don't talk to or see anyone until after 4 p.m., when my brain seems to shut off for the day. Or when my mental health is suffering, I spend a lot more time in nature and with the people and dogs who want to be out there with me. But when you're not suffering—when you're just living your life and trying to take the next right step—the simplest truth that I think we sometimes forget in this individualistic world of ours is, life isn't just about you. Maintaining our social media profiles has made it seem like we need to prove we can go it alone, and more and more people swapping careers for the gig economy makes it feel as though we *are* alone. Growing movements like minimalism feel pretty individualistic too. But we are wired for connection. And when you're venturing into the unknown, shutting yourself off from new people risks *everyone* missing out on the opportunity to connect with someone in a meaningful or memorable way.

While taking a new path might feel like a personal journey you need to lead the way on, if you keep your eyes open, you'll find a lot of people who are on their own journeys too. You might be doing things differently, but you've probably walked away from people who don't understand you or maybe even discouraged you from doing what felt right. And as you continue down these paths, you could lose even more people along the way. So when you cross paths with someone new, remember that you can both provide some comfort simply by acknowledging each other's presence.

You won't know which interactions are going to be the most meaningful. Sometimes you'll meet someone once and that will be good enough. And sometimes you'll meet someone a second or third time, and it will just keep getting better and better. Maybe they'll even become your new best friend over time. But they don't have to. Nobody needs that kind of pressure. So don't try to figure it out during that first greeting, or worry about where your friendship/relationship could go. Just remember that if you meet people who seem to understand what you are doing or who you are becoming, make time for them. At the very least, say *hello*.

Enjoy the View

When you finally get on a path that's right for you, you should feel the benefits right from the start. Like when you give up foods that always made you bloated and quickly notice how much more comfortable you are in your body. Or when you take a break from social media and realize how much more time you have for the things you always said you wanted to do. Or when you move to a new city or town and enjoy the stage of exploring and falling in love with your new home. That's not to say that the early days don't also come with challenges. Of course they do. But you made a choice for yourself that you hoped would be a positive one. If that's proving to be true, you're allowed to enjoy it. I would even argue that you should.

In Western society, it sometimes feels as though everything is supposed to be a struggle. Not just because the world is in trouble and our society is to blame for many of the issues we are facing (I'll leave that topic for other authors to write about), but also because it's culturally normal. It's normal to complain about your work, your commitments, your family, and your friends. And it's normal to complain about not having enough time to do what you really want to do. If you *don't* complain about these things, you're probably already used to being the odd one out. People notice the one employee who always seems to be happy at work, or the one person who seems genuinely thrilled every time her extended family pops by unannounced. Choosing to be happy, therefore, isn't the cultural norm. Choosing to complain is. To "enjoy the view" of your life, then, isn't just a radical act. It's something you may not have a lot of practice doing! I hear this whenever I listen to my friends talk about the next goal they are going to work toward, without ever stopping to acknowledge how much progress they've made at something. And I see it all the time when I'm in the outdoors.

At some point in the beginning stage of a hike, you should reach a sort of viewpoint. Sometimes it's clearly marked and may even have a bench for you to sit on. Other times, it's more like a clearing in the trees or an opening of the path. Whatever shape it comes in, if you look for it, you shouldn't miss it. Because this viewpoint is giving you a first glimpse of what you're walking toward — of why you're doing this.

How you choose to enjoy the view is entirely up to you. Alanna, of course, taught me how to smile and take more deep breaths at the viewpoint. Pascal and I often get so excited that we start singing songs from our favorite childhood movies. (If her kids are with us, we sing even louder in hopes of embarrassing them. The things I never knew would bring me such joy as an adult!) Thanks to them both, I do these things even when I'm hiking by myself. And if I'm completely alone at a viewpoint, I will also happily holler into the wind: *Wooooo!* I'm not saying you have to do any of those things when you're in the outdoors or when you're opting out. What I am suggesting is that you take a moment to acknowledge where you're at. It took a lot for you to even step onto this path, let alone start walking down it. Now you're here. You're doing it! And it feels good! So let it feel good.

Going back to Brooke's story: after she started decluttering her home, she began filling some of the empty space with plants. Then more plants and more plants. Not a jungle of them. Just little bits of greenery that made her house feel more alive. It didn't take long for Brooke to notice she was enjoying her home again. That she actually liked the white space. (A viewpoint!) She liked the empty walls. (Another viewpoint!) She liked her new plants, and how they inspired her to get outside and into the garden. (Viewpoints all around!) But she was surprised to realize she wasn't alone. It wasn't just Brooke and Ben who were happier at their home now. Once they started making these changes, other people seemed to like spending time there too. Brooke and Ben started entertaining more. Hosted Christmases and Easters and barbecues. And even more interesting to Brooke was the fact that her introverted self was actually enjoying it all. (A major viewpoint.)

This is when Brooke realized that she was onto something. That what she'd started was about so much more than just decluttering. It wasn't about clearing out cupboards or cleaning out the garage. She and Ben were consciously creating the home they wanted. And while it wasn't what other people in her life might have created for themselves, *everyone* was enjoying the view.

So please: take the time to appreciate what it feels like to be on your new path. Don't just take the next step or try to rush to the summit. If you don't stop to enjoy the views along the way, then your only memory of the adventure will be that you did what you intended to do. But you won't remember any of the beautiful moments that made it so meaningful. And you will want to be able to draw on that stuff later—especially when things get harder, which I can guarantee they will.

Look Both Ways

The first solo hike I ever did in Squamish was a quick and steep climb off the side of the highway. It offers the same views people get when they push themselves up the Stawamus Chief, which is the most popular hike among both locals and visitors, but in a fraction of the time. And if you take one route in particular, you will discover a secret: the initial viewpoint offers the exact same view as what you will see when you get all the way to the summit. Which is to say: if you're tired, or simply aren't in the mood to do the full thing, you have the opportunity to stop and turn around here.

When you're opting out, there are a number of reasons you might consider turning around at the metaphorical viewpoint. One that isn't talked about enough (if at all!) in the self-help space is that you might not be happy with the direction this new path is taking you. We buy and read self-help books, skim blogs, et cetera, because we think we want to do what they are prescribing, but the reality is that it might not actually be the right choice for us. The lifestyle changes, the new movements, or the popular trends don't work for everyone because we are all different to begin with. So if every step has felt like a struggle and you feel miserable, you are allowed to change your mind. Especially if you haven't even caught a glimpse of the viewpoint, or of what the positive benefits of making this change might be for you. It's okay if this new path isn't actually one you want to be on. You can stop here, and you don't owe anyone an explanation as to why.

I talked about this idea with my friend David Cain. He has been conducting experiments on himself since 2009 and documenting the results on his blog, *Raptitude*. When we were looking through the full list of experiments on his website, we talked about which ones were successful and which ones weren't. During our discussion, David realized that the successful experiments were the ones where he saw some immediate progress. He saw a reason to keep going. That doesn't mean there weren't challenges. All his successful experiments demanded that he change a behavior or some part of his mindset, which is never easy. The successful ones were just the ones that showed him it was going to be worth doing the work. He was happy with the path they were leading him down.

Another reason you might stop here, then, could be that you're not willing to do that work. And that's okay too sometimes. The viewpoint offers a brief moment of elation, when you can look back at what you've done so far and see where it has led you—and then you can also look ahead and see that it's going to take a lot more time and effort to reach the summit. I do have a theory that it's easy to quit something after you've made any amount of progress, and that this is why so many people never take all the steps required to change their lives. But it is also true that your path is going to come with challenges. You're going to sweat. It might even hurt. Are you still willing and motivated to do that work? Or do you want to turn around now? Take a long pause here—as much time as you need to make an intentional decision versus submit to an impulsive reaction.

With travel, there was no doubt in my mind that I wanted to keep going on this adventure. The first few weeks of my time in the UK were better than I had imagined. Relaxing in Brighton. Hiking with Meg. Spending time with Kate. Connecting with Chris. And then reconnecting with old friends in London, and getting to spend some proper quality time with them. It felt so much better than my first UK visit. The slower pace meant I didn't have to rush around. It allowed me to settle into a new neighborhood in the city, and get to know it in a way I couldn't have if I had spent only two nights there. I worked in the mornings and then allocated entire afternoons to rambling in coffee shops with Chris, and wandering new areas with my friend Bianca. I was also cooking and walking and running, and taking care of myself in general. I knew there would be challenges ahead, but this felt good. I felt solid. So there was no question about whether or not I would keep going. I was here, and I was doing this.

What would feel good for you today? This is a question my friend Azalea Moen asks me often, but especially when we are on a trip together. It's a reminder that we each get to have input into how our day goes, and individually we get to pick something that feels right for us. I often think about her question when I'm traveling alone, and I try to ask myself a similar one when I'm standing at a juncture. *Does this feel like the right path for me?* If the answer is no, I will either pivot or turn around. And if the answer is yes, I proceed. I can't answer that question for you. I don't know if it feels good, or if it feels as though you're on the right path. Only you can know what the next right step is. Just promise me you won't continue in order to prove anything to anyone else. Carry on only if that's what feels right for you. No matter which direction you go, I hope you will choose to believe there is more ahead for you in life, because there is. There will always be more paths to take.

SECTION 3

The Valley

If you decide to keep going and to continue your adventure in opting out, here's what's going to happen next. Your journey is going to be surprising. It's going to be rewarding. And it's going to be hard. If you didn't quit and turn around at the viewpoint, you will probably be tempted to at some point in the near future. At the very least, there will come a time when you will find yourself feeling lost and unsure of how to move forward. That's what happens when you enter the valley.

A valley is a low area of land between two mountains. Less commonly known as a vale, it can be home to some of the most beautiful sights on your journey. But if you're hiking into a valley from a viewpoint, you can't help but think about the fact that every step down is going to need to be a step up later. The farther down you go, the taller the trees and mountains seem to grow all around you. And when you get to the bottom, staring back up at them has a way of making you feel as though you're surrounded by impossible feats.

Most of what you "packed" or prepared for this adventure will be needed in the valley. But you will also learn that you couldn't prepare for some of the situations you will find yourself in, because you didn't know they were coming. Of course you didn't. You've never been here or tried to live this way before.

Not surprisingly, then, walking through the valley isn't easy. It can be extremely uncomfortable, especially if what you've opted out of was a coping mechanism before. It leaves you vulnerable to the elements, and pushes you to grow at an accelerated speed. It's where you could lose sight of the path, and lose sight of some of the people who used to walk alongside you. To get through it, you have to sit in the discomfort. Find new ways to cope and take care of yourself. Be willing to walk away from relationships that aren't working anymore and also willing to shed part of yourself that is no longer serving you. And you will have to use your senses to guide you back to the path and keep moving in the direction you want to go.

No matter how much we wish we could, we can't skip this part. We can't leap from the viewpoint to the summit of a hike. And we can't keep leaving it out of self-help books either. We can't just write an introduction that sells an idea and a conclusion about how amazing your life will be after you embrace said idea. We have to talk about what happens in the middle. Because the middle is where you are going to face some of your biggest challenges. If you do what you've always done, you'll get where you've always gone — and I know that's not what you want.

The valley has looked different and lasted for a different length of time with every opt-out I've done. When I decided to stop drinking, I think I was living in the valley for close to two years after the viewpoint (which I had reached after just a few months of sobriety, when I was taking much better care of my physical health). That valley came with some dark moments. The well-versed voice in my head seemed to know I was struggling with something in my life and tried to talk me into drinking again. I shared a couple of those stories in my first book.

When moving to a new city, I'm typically in the valley for a few months. It's right after the honeymoon phase of being excited and getting settled in, but before I've found a community or made any friends. With something like deleting a social media account, it looks different still: there are usually only a couple of weeks (or even days) when the fear of missing out is realized and I wonder if I've made a mistake.

With long-term travel, the valley I entered in my first year wasn't as painful as some of the others I've experienced. It also wasn't particularly dramatic. But remember when I said stories don't need to be movie-worthy in order to be told? That's because most of us are never going to live through them. They might make a great movie, but they aren't always relatable—and we need the relatable stories so we can figure out how to work through the challenges that come up in our own lives. That's why this story feels more important to share with you. I started off confident and assumed I could handle any situation that came up. But that assumption quickly took me down a path I wasn't prepared for, which could have led to an even quicker failure. In a way, it was a failure. As you'll see, I failed to do what I originally set out to do. This valley also taught me lessons that I didn't want to learn, and I discovered things about myself that I didn't want to be true. Fortunately, I didn't actually lose anyone this time—but I did have to have some tough conversations and speak up for myself in a way that I hadn't before.

You might not go through the exact same situation, but my guess is you'll share similar feelings on your journey. So I can't tell you exactly what's going to happen in your valley, but it is my responsibility to tell you to be ready for it. Because you can't plan for everything, but you can and should expect that you're going to find yourself in situations you don't know how to navigate. It's not really an adventure until something goes wrong.

Downhill

You would think that the ascent on a mountain might be the most difficult part of the journey. You're sweating, panting, and breathing heavily—and because you can't always see the top, it feels as though the climb is never going to end. For me personally, though, going down is often harder than going up. You might not sweat going down. And your breathing is fairly calm, for the most part. But staying upright on the down slope requires more core strength. You might need to change your strategy and walk sideways, or crouch so you're lower to the ground, in order to remain steady. And if any of your muscles were shaky on the way up, they will be even more so on the way down.

In mid-April, I left London and took the train out to Frome, in Somerset, to visit Fiona. Fiona was another friend I'd made simply by saying hello just a few weeks before my very first trip to the UK in 2018. After our mutual friend, Jen, shared one of Fiona's articles, I went down the rabbit hole of her blog and felt I'd found a long-lost sister across the pond. This became especially true when I read the description for her podcast, *There Are Other Ways*. It was "for people brave enough to explore a less well-trodden path in life." We were speaking the same language. I signed up for her email newsletter and then received her automated welcome email, which included a list of books she'd recently read and loved—and *The Year of Less* was at the top. Of course I had to respond.

Within our early email exchanges I told Fiona I was coming to the UK for the first time, and she invited me to stay with her for a couple of nights. I've found that these kinds of offers are often made by people who have opted out in some way. It's as if we all secretly know that everyone needs extra kindness and generosity when they're "living life a little differently," as Fiona would say. So we step into our roles as fellow adventure partners and hold out our hands to help each other get where we want to go.

During that first visit, Fiona and I connected on some point with every topic that came up. The work we did and the work we wanted to do, the places we'd been and the places we wanted to go, the books we'd recently enjoyed, and what it was like to be single in our thirties. We shared an appreciation for the outdoors, and for living quieter lives in smaller cities. And when it was time for me to go, we both agreed we hoped our paths would cross again one day.

When I decided to practice slow travel long term and booked a flight back to the UK, Fiona was one of the first people I told. This time, she offered to put me up for a week—and over Easter, so I would have someone to spend the holiday weekend with. Two acts of kindness wrapped into one.

Taking the train from London felt a little bit like coming home this time. Like driving from Vancouver up the mountains and into Squamish. The rail line served as my British version of the Sea-to-Sky Highway, taking me away from the busy city center and out into a quiet town surrounded by the countryside. In Frome, Fiona's and my days were filled with work, walks, and visits to her new allotment (a plot in a community garden). The warm spring weather allowed us to have picnics outside her front door and even eat our Easter lunch on the patio of a local inn. We spent time at her friends' coffee shop, and met some of the many young creatives who make up the community Fiona loves. And on one of my last days in Frome, we went down to Dorset and hiked from Lulworth Cove, past Durdle Door, and all the way over to Weymouth — twelve miles of rolling hills, white cliffs against turquoise waters, and rocky beaches. I should have been having an incredible time. And I was — at least during the day. But at night I was spending hours staring into the shallow depths of my laptop screen, searching for something that no longer seemed to exist.

The affordable long-term rentals I had once found had vanished from the internet. When I plugged the cities and dates into my search options, nothing was coming up in my price range. I tried to play around with the dates, hoping that might change the prices. Still nothing. So I expanded my budget ever so slightly, then ever so slightly again, and then ever so slightly yet again, until I learned the truth. Every rental in the cities I'd been thinking of staying in now seemed to be at least $500 to $1,000 Canadian over my monthly budget. At *least*. Some of the cities' cheapest rentals were $1,500 Canadian over my original budget. And none of these were options for me. I could maybe stomach going $500 Canadian over budget for one month, but that would have to be one heck of a home and in one heck of a place. Anyway, the point wasn't to go to a new city and just enjoy the home I was staying in. I wanted to go out and explore the city! To walk around, find a great coffee shop to work in, visit museums, read books in the park, try to connect with a few locals, and so on. I also wanted to be able to catch a train once a week or so and go hiking somewhere new. If I increased my budget by too much, I wouldn't be able to afford any of that. And at the end of the day, it would still give me a place to live for only one month.

The more time I spent searching, the more I began to realize that I might have made a huge mistake. Before I left Canada, I had done just enough research to figure out which cities in the UK might be the most affordable ones to stay in, but I hadn't actually booked anything. Instead, I'd made plans to travel around and stay with friends for the first month, and I figured I would book places once I was over there. If you had asked me how I felt about that decision before I left home, I would have told you I was fine with it. I had an open and flexible mindset about it all and trusted that I could figure everything out from the road. But the further I went with this search on the internet, the more impossible — and unaffordable — it started to feel. I might not be able to stay in any of the cities I'd originally intended. I might not be able to stay in the UK at all. I had no idea what I was going to do, but this whole adventure suddenly felt as though it was going to be a lot harder than I'd imagined when I first set out. Things were quickly going downhill, and I did not have the core strength or backup strategy prepared to deal with it.

The Backcountry

Depending on what part of the world you're in, the word "backcountry" can mean a number of different things. In some countries, it's used to describe land that isn't accessible to the public: you might need permission from the landowner to cross it, or it might be entirely off-limits. In North America, the word is used to describe land that is remote and largely undeveloped. You can absolutely head out there and explore it. But you may not find clear paths, and certainly no trail markers. If you choose to venture into the backcountry, it's entirely up to you to navigate your way in, around, and back out. Beyond having a general sense of direction, you need to go in prepared for any outcome. And you should definitely expect the unexpected.

When I was living in Squamish, I met a lot of experienced backcountry explorers. On their days off from work, they would pack their bags and load their 4x4s with bikes or skis and set off to see what the world had in store for them. To enter the backcountry, you will typically start off on a marked path or road. Eventually, you get to a place where the path just disappears, or the paved road turns to unmaintained gravel or dirt, and you have to decide where you want to go next. You are truly in the wilderness. It's an outdoor enthusiast's playground. A wide-open space with endless directions to go in and possibilities for what you will do or see. But if you're not experienced or prepared, it can be an extremely overwhelming—and vulnerable—place to find yourself.

Personally, even though I'm fairly confident in my sense of direction, I am still not at a place where I feel comfortable with the idea of exploring the backcountry by myself. But when it comes to opting out, I have enough experience to tell you this: if you go deep enough into the valley, at some point you are going to find yourself in the backcountry of your own adventure. You will take one misstep, or something will happen that causes you to lose sight of what you are trying to do, and you will look down and see that the new path you were on has suddenly disappeared. Every step then takes you deeper into the wilderness, and you won't be prepared. You can't be prepared for how to handle it because you have no experience with this new way of life. Without a path beneath your feet, you could find yourself scrambling to find one. And while the options around you are seemingly endless, which some people might say sounds exciting, this could also create an overwhelming sensation that ultimately ruins the whole experience.

This sense of losing the new path you were on can be sparked by so many different things. A comment from someone you love or respect that makes you question everything you're trying to do. A relapse or slipup that makes you think about how much easier it might be to just go back to your old way of life. Or a simple enough mistake that leads you to feel like a failure. It doesn't take much to trigger more fear, especially if you were already somewhat apprehensive about walking into the unknown.

I thought I had enough experience with this to be prepared for when and how it might come up again in my own adventures in opting out. But by not booking any places to stay before leaving home, I had essentially forced myself to walk straight into the backcountry at the start — and I didn't realize this until I was in it. Or rather until I found myself sitting on Fiona's couch night after night, looking for affordable places to stay and coming up with nothing.

I shared my struggles with her, essentially waving my white flag and calling in the help of a fellow adventurer. And *bless her,* as the Brits would say, she really tried to help me find different options. On that first night of my realization, Fiona started listing cities in the UK that I hadn't thought of and suggested I see what average prices for long-term rentals were there. When all those proved to be just as expensive, she asked me where else I wanted to go. We spent the next few nights pulling each country's Lonely Planet travel guide from the collection on her bookshelf and skimming through it. Fiona had done a lot of solo travel and shared incredible (and cost-saving) tips on navigating some of her favorite cities in Europe. When all my dream cities, plus the ones she loved, were also deemed to be over my budget, I changed my strategy. I flipped the equation and started searching for homes by price rather than by destination. Then I widened the map over entire countries to see what came up. This helped me write a list of cities I'd never thought of but ultimately didn't really want to visit.

Every option I discussed with Fiona gave me hope that I would find something. I saw a little glimmer of what each direction I could go in would look like and wondered: *Is this a path? Is that a path? Is this the path for me?* But as each one turned out to not be viable, I started to feel more and more lost. As if I was stuck in the middle of the vast wilderness and didn't know how to navigate my way out of it. I didn't even know what I wanted anymore, other than that I desperately wanted this idea of slowly traveling all year to actually work.

By the time I left Frome, I still hadn't booked any homes. It was April 23. I was house-sitting for Saima in London until May 1 and then I was staying with my friend Jess in the Peak District for two more nights. That gave me ten days to find my first long-term rental. I wish I could say that I still felt hopeful, but my sense of adventure was slowly draining. I was exhausted—and I was beginning to notice that I was growing uncomfortable with another issue too.

Internal Compass

My dad—a lifelong sailor—will laugh when he reads this, but I didn't know how to read a compass until I was in my early thirties. Up until then, I thought that if I simply held it out and the arrow was pointing in any one direction, then that must be the direction it was pointing to. I'm so thankful I never ventured into the backcountry with that knowledge, because it would have guided me in the wrong direction—fast—and likely taken me to a location I would've had no idea how to navigate my way out of.

Without writing a full technical explanation of how to properly read a compass, I will just say that you have to start by figuring out which direction north is. Once you know that, you can see where south, east, and west are (and all the inter-cardinal and secondary intercardinal points in between). But it always comes back to north. If you don't know how to find that, you won't know where to go.

The purpose of a compass is twofold. Of course, if you get lost, it helps you navigate your way back to a starting or safety point. But it also helps guide you in the right direction from the beginning, when you're trying to get somewhere you've never been before. For this reason, I will always recommend that you pack a physical compass in your bag (once you've actually learned how to read it) before going on any kind of big outdoor adventure. It's also a good idea to check in with your *internal* compass before you leave on any adventure and as you continue down the path.

In the outdoors, your internal compass can be used to remind you *why* you're doing a particular hike. What you want to see, who you want to go with (or if you want to go solo), how long you want to be out there, the pace you want to move at, and how you want to feel. Essentially, it will remind you to check in with yourself and make sure you're having the experience you had intended — or, if it has shifted, an experience that still feels good for you. And if you care about the land you'll be walking on, you can also use your internal compass to make sure you're respecting it.

When it comes to opting out, your internal compass can be a term used to describe your *values*. Your values are essentially the personal code of conduct or morals that you choose to live by. Being able to identify your values is arguably one of the most important parts of living an intentional life. It's also one of the most difficult concepts to explain, especially if you've never before consciously thought about what yours might be. I certainly hadn't. And personally, it wasn't until I started to recognize what it felt like to be living *out* of alignment with my values that I began to figure out what they actually were.

One of the first times I can remember this happening was right before I made the decision to stop smoking weed. I was twenty-five years old and had done a lot of work to change the direction my life was going in. One of the most important steps I had taken was to go back to school and finish my degree in communications. I continued to smoke weed throughout the first year of my two-year program but slowly started to notice some things I didn't like about my daily life. I was often tired and made the excuse that it was okay for me to waste many evenings on the couch. (*I'm not lazy. I'm relaxing and taking care of myself!*) I also couldn't seem to focus on things for very long. This resulted in assignments and deadlines stacking up, which made my anxiety climb right alongside them.

And then one day I was finally willing to accept that smoking weed was the culprit. These weren't just signs that I needed to opt out of it (though they were that too). They were signs that I was living out of alignment with one of my values, which at the time was to further my education. I was paying to get this degree, and it mattered to me. But smoking weed was getting in the way of me living the life I wanted. As soon as I realized it, I stopped—and the lazy behavior, and the *excuses* for my lazy behavior, disappeared. It wasn't easy to then, in turn, opt out of some of the friendships I had with people I used to get high with, but I finally felt as though I was going in the right direction after that.

Many of my opt-outs have led to similar moments of realization partway through. I've started down a new path, then tripped over an old habit or story in my head, and lost sight of what I was working toward. I don't always notice what's wrong at first, but there's a general sense that something is off. And something definitely felt off for me as I was finishing up my first month in the UK.

When I first made the decision to attempt to travel long term, I didn't want to talk about it publicly. For starters, I have never been comfortable with the idea of glorifying travel. It's both a privilege and also a difficult way to live. Exciting and scary. Fulfilling and lonely. Beautiful and sometimes dark. And for those reasons, and all the nuances in between, I have never wanted to promote it as a path everyone should take. Since I was choosing it for myself, though, I came up with a short list of rules that I wanted to live by.

One of them was to not create more waste than I would have at home. If you don't plan properly, travel has a way of being extremely wasteful, and I hated the idea of creating more waste than I needed to—especially in a country that belonged to other people. Unfortunately, this proved to be a nearly impossible feat since every time I walked into a grocery store in the UK, everything seemed to be wrapped in plastic. The produce aisle was the most difficult to navigate. Compared to North America, where produce is placed in open bins, everything in the UK was packaged. Apples, bananas, broccoli, lettuce—all in plastic bags. I hated it. Eventually, I started looking for farmer's markets, but their dates didn't always line up with when I was in a particular city. So right from the start, I was creating more waste than I would have at home, which made me uncomfortable every time I shopped.

Beyond the waste factor, though, shortly after I returned to the UK, I noticed something a little more concerning: I wasn't as comfortable with the idea of *flying* anymore. Hopping on planes and traveling from place to place—it started to make me feel both anxious and immoral. Both of these discomforts stemmed from my awareness of the growing movement around the importance of addressing climate change. And this makes sense, especially since I was in the UK, where Extinction Rebellion had been launched the year before, protests were getting bigger and happening more frequently, and climate change was discussed a lot more seriously in the media than it was, as I recalled, back in Canada.

Before I left home, I knew that one of my values was mindful consumption, which is why I had decided I didn't want to create a lot of waste on the road. But after learning that flying had such a horrendous impact on global warming, I realized that my values were shifting further. I know I've said this already, but once you see things, you can't unsee them—and I could not unsee the statistics I was reading about flying. Or forget the people I was meeting in the UK who were committing to never fly again. It wasn't a political statement or a hill I wanted to die on, per se. And I wasn't yet prepared to make the decision to never get on another plane in my life. I just knew that I didn't feel great about it anymore. And I wasn't sure how to address this shift in my values—especially now that I had already started this new adventure of mine.

I first shared this feeling with Fiona when she and I were searching for different cities I could stay in all across Europe. We used this information to change the search and try to find cities that were more easily accessible by train. But when those cities, too, turned out to be outside my budget, I started to wonder how I had gotten here. How my internal compass— and my values—had shifted so drastically. Now, looking back, I can see it might have been a good thing that I wasn't locked into any long-term rentals in destinations that would have required a lot of travel. But you can't always see the silver lining when you're in the thick of change. I was only a few weeks into this, and I was already so far off the path I had thought I wanted to take. I did not know how to move forward.

There are a lot of articles and books that say you can't live an intentional life until you know what your values are, and I do believe that's true. But whereas most other writers will give you the same exercise to help you determine what your values are, I'm hesitant to suggest that reading a list of a hundred words and circling five or ten will be helpful. In my earliest experiences with that exercise, before I had developed much self-awareness, I found I picked words that described either my aspirations (the things I hoped to value one day) or the values my parents had. And both of these things make sense: we are shaped by people, places, and culture. But that doesn't mean all those values have to feel good or right for you. They certainly don't for me today.

Years ago, I never could've told you that I would value the things I do today. A few of the words that come up for me right now are "slow," "presence," "learning," and "growth." And based on some of the experiments I've done and things I've learned from those, "mindful consumption" and "the environment" are on that list too. I didn't grow up having these values instilled in me, though. For that reason, it hasn't been (and still isn't always) easy to show up fully as myself in all situations. It's not easy to talk about something you're only just starting to think about. It's not easy to challenge the values your family has, or to do things differently than they would. It's not easy to know how to live in alignment with your values if nobody has modeled this for you.

In fact, you may not be able to figure out what your values are *until* you're living out of alignment with them. To look at the way you are living and ask yourself how you feel about it. To pay attention to the things that don't feel good. If you're living out of alignment with any of your values, you know. It can leave you feeling sad, disconnected from reality, guilty, ashamed, and so on. And it can leave you feeling stuck. Because if you aren't letting your internal compass guide you, you won't know which direction is north, and you will eventually get lost on the path. This is what happened to me, even after I thought I had figured out what my values were before I left home.

S.T.O.P.

I'm terrified of getting lost in the outdoors. It hasn't happened to me yet, but that's probably only because one near encounter was enough to teach me to always go in prepared, pay attention to my surroundings, and trust my gut. And looking back now, I can see that my near miss was bound to happen from the start.

I have always preferred to go hiking first thing in the morning. This is partially out of necessity because the parking lots near the trailheads fill up early in British Columbia. But it's also a safety measure: the earlier you go, the more daylight hours you have to explore. On this particular day, I'd had no intention of going for a hike. However, after finding myself in an argument, I couldn't shake off the feeling that I needed to release some of the tension in my body. I decided to get some fresh air.

It was midafternoon on a late-fall day and I decided to do the hike closest to me in Port Moody. This was a lake I'd been around many times before, so I knew the main path well. But about an hour into it, when I approached one of the side paths,

I decided to finally take it. To stop wondering where it would lead and just go see for myself. The first few steps on this path felt spontaneous and exciting. *I was trying something new! And going to see new things!* But as I climbed farther up, I realized I wasn't really getting anywhere. I was still just going up a hill, surrounded by trees and with no sign of what I was walking toward. I didn't look at what time I decided to take this new path, so I wasn't sure how long I'd been hiking, but it felt like at least thirty minutes. And then I noticed how dark it was getting among the trees. The sun was starting to go down.

My reaction, in this moment, was automatic: I had to turn around and go back to the main path. It would likely take me ninety minutes to get back to my car, and I now knew I would be walking through the dark for at least part of that time. Remember when I said that I was terrified of getting lost in the outdoors? Let me tell you now that I think my biggest fear is walking alone in the dark. Even when I'm walking along main streets in a city, if it's dark out, I will often call a friend or at least send Emma some audio messages that describe where I am and what time I should arrive at my destination. It's the only thing that makes me feel safe because my anxious mind runs wild when I'm alone in the dark.

As soon as I turned around, my adrenaline kicked in and I all but raced down the hill. Back on the main path, I felt safer. It was familiar territory, and I should've been confident in my ability to get back to my car. All I had to do was retrace my steps. But as it got darker, I got more anxious. Every sound caused me to panic and imagine that something or someone was going to "get me." *Was that just a small bird fluttering through a shrub? Or a snake? Or a bear? Or someone looking through the shrub and deciding whether they wanted to jump*

out and attack me? My heart started pounding and I was holding my breath—something I often do when I'm afraid that
only makes my anxiety spike further. I quickened my steps
and nearly started to run. Then, as soon as my view started to
go completely black, I saw the trailhead and found my car
parked almost right next to it.

While I didn't get fully lost that day, I have since learned
that there is a useful acronym included in all survival manuals
outlining what to do if you ever find yourself in that situation:
S.T.O.P.

- S: Stop—Literally stop where you are. Continuing on
  will only risk getting you lost further, especially if you're
  panicking and not paying attention to your surroundings. So stop. Maybe even sit down. Just do whatever
  will help you calm down and feel grounded in this place.
- T: Think—While remaining seated/standing in place,
  think about where you might be and how you got here.
  Which direction did you come from? How long have you
  been hiking? How are you on resources (water, food,
  time, sunlight hours, et cetera)? What do you remember
  reading about this hike that could help you?
- O: Observe—If you have a compass/map or working
  GPS, pull them out and try to figure out where you are.
  If you don't have any of those things, look around and try
  to reorient yourself. Can you see any notable landmarks
  around you that might signal which way you should go?
  What is the last landmark or memorable thing you
  remember seeing?
- P: Plan—Don't take another step until you've come up
  with a plan. If you're confident you can navigate your

way out of the situation, do that. But if you're not confident, remain where you are. You have a better chance of being found if you stay put rather than going deeper into the wilderness and farther away from the people who could rescue you.

Without knowing I was doing so at the time, I quickly ran through these four steps when I realized I wasn't going to be able to complete my hike in Port Moody. I stopped (for only a few moments), realized I was running out of time and daylight, looked to see that I was still on a clearly marked path that could take me back to my car, and started heading down toward it. Years later, I ran through these steps again when I realized I wasn't getting anywhere with my travel planning.

On my train back to London, I realized just how lost I was on this journey. Nothing about it felt good anymore. I wasn't confident in the path I had taken. I didn't know where I was going. I didn't even know what the goal was at this point. *Why was I doing any of this?!* My anxiety had taken control of my thoughts, and they were constantly spiraling. I was running on adrenaline, searching online, thinking about every possible scenario, and hoping to find a simple solution—but there wasn't one. Or at least not one that I could see clearly. So I S.T.O.P. 'd:

- Stop—When I got to Saima's apartment, I decided to take a few days off to assess my situation and come up with a plan. I didn't go out or do anything to distract myself. I just bought a couple of bags of groceries, settled into her home, and tried to calm my anxious mind.

- Think—I thought about my original intention for this trip, and what it had quickly shaped into instead. And then I assessed my resources—specifically, my money—and knew I was in some trouble. I could make this work temporarily, but I could also waste a lot of money trying to stay on this current path.
- Observe—I checked in with my internal compass and asked myself how I was feeling. The first emotion was fear. Mostly, the fear of quitting and feeling like a failure. But when I was really honest with myself, I also felt guilt over being completely out of alignment with my values, and that felt worse.
- Plan—After a few days, I could see only two options: I could book an expensive place for one month and spend that time looking for more affordable places, or I could book a flight home. Neither option was the clear winner, but we can't take two paths at the same time. In the end, we have to choose one.

The foolish thing would have been for me to keep going on that hike in Port Moody. To keep pushing myself up that new path and hoping I could find my way. I would have loved to have seen what was up there, but it wasn't a safe option. My safest bet was to retrace my steps that day—and that's what I decided to do on this adventure too. I would turn around on this path, retrace my steps, and go back home, taking all the lessons I needed to learn back with me. And when I was ready, I would come up with a revised adventure and try opting out again.

Change Course

There are a lot of reasons you might quit a hike partway through. Running low on resources (like water) is one. Injuring yourself and not having any first aid materials or experience is another. If you don't feel prepared to tackle some part of the terrain, you will know when it's time to stop. You are also at the mercy of Mother Nature out there. If the weather changes in a dramatic way (too hot, too cold, too much rain/ snow, et cetera), you should take it as a sign and head back to the trailhead.

This isn't going to happen on all your adventures in opting out. It may not happen on any of them. But I've started and stopped enough of these experiments myself that I feel I can say this with all certainty: if you change your plans partway through, it's going to hurt. It's going to be hard to make that decision. It's going to feel like a struggle to turn around and hike back out, knowing you didn't accomplish what you set out to do. The weight of your backpack will somehow feel heavier, even if it's technically lighter. It's going to feel even heavier if you're carrying it home to family or friends who might have been less than supportive of your decision to try to opt out in the first place.

I don't see any point in sugarcoating this part of the process. The fear of "failing" is already one of the reasons so many of us don't try to change our lives. If you had the courage to try anyway, that means you technically knew this was a possibility. But even if you knew it could happen, that doesn't mean you will be fully prepared for how to handle it. So we need to talk about what happens when you do—when you change direction or change your mind altogether. Because if you pushed past the viewpoint but then couldn't reach the summit, you are going to experience the steep range of emotions that come with backtracking your steps.

Drinking is the clearest example of something I stopped and started countless times. I even publicly declared that I was going to stop a few of those times—but then always went back to it (until I didn't). With the shopping ban, I never "failed," but I talked myself into an impulse purchase once and broke the ban. I didn't sweep it under the rug. I wrote a blog post about what I had learned and included that same story in my first book. I also changed the rules a few months later, when I realized my values were shifting throughout that first year—and again I shared my writing on the subject publicly. And I set out to do a thirty-day social media detox once and quit on day twenty-two. That decision was very intentional, and I didn't feel bad about it at all. We had to put down our family dog, Molly, that day, and I wanted to write something for her. That felt more important than seeing what would happen if I spent another eight days off-line. I didn't have to prove myself to anyone. I had learned enough to know that.

Looking back at those examples, I can now see a slow and natural progression in my decision-making process. Today, if I decide to change plans partway through an opt-out, it's very intentional. I know it's not a failure, and that I am not a failure. I've learned that it's perfectly okay to try something new and figure out that it's not the right choice for you. Or that it might feel right for a few months or even years, but that doesn't mean it has to feel right forever. When we make a choice, we don't have to choose it for the rest of our lives. If you don't finish the hike, you're still better off for having tried. So now, no matter when or why I decide to stop something or change directions on my journey, I will always be glad I tried and get to take some lessons with me into the future as a result. In my earliest adventures, though, my decisions weren't intentional at all. Going back on my decision to opt out of something wasn't really the right choice for me. I was self-sabotaging.

Self-sabotaging is essentially any action you take that stops you from achieving a goal you set for yourself. And you do these things when you have conflicting thoughts about what you are trying to do. So one part of you wants to try something new, but the other is afraid of change. You want to be sober, but you like that you're known as a fun person to party with. You want to be a vegetarian or even go vegan, but you're tired of hearing comments about it from family or friends. So you drink the drink or eat the meat and stay on the path you know. Sometimes that's because it feels easier to stick to what's familiar, but more often than not it's because it's simply easier to stick to the identity we know. The words used to describe us as kids, or that made us feel good as adults, can be hard to let go of. This is one of the reasons it's so hard to let go of your former self. Personally, I also sabotaged a few changes I was trying to make because I just didn't like myself enough to believe I deserved to succeed.

One of the reasons that deciding to go home early from my UK trip was so hard was because I really didn't want to do it. It didn't feel like the right choice. So I had to constantly check in with myself and make sure I wasn't sabotaging the idea that I might be able to travel long term. That I wasn't going to permanently change course and walk away from this thing I wanted. That I wasn't going to give up on myself. Because I knew what could happen if I felt as though I had failed or as though I was throwing in the towel. I could end up going down a long shame spiral that would ultimately lead to some kind of self-destructive behavior—and I was not interested in that.

While working through these feelings on my own, I ended up listening a handful of times to an interview Gale did with Nicole on Gale's *She Explores* podcast. In the episode, titled "Quitting Is a Kindness," Nicole tells the story of how she set out to hike the Pacific Crest Trail southbound from Canada to Mexico in 2018. After eighty-six days, she decided to stop in Northern California—1,600 miles into her 2,600-mile hike. Her insomnia was hurting her yet again, and she knew that getting off-trail was the smartest decision she could make for her body and mind. After announcing her decision to quit, Nicole noticed that all her Instagram followers were quick to chime in that she wasn't failing: she was simply doing what was right for her. While this was true, Nicole felt it was also true that she had failed. She had set out to hike the Pacific Crest Trail and she couldn't finish it in one go. Technically, she failed.

I realized I had to accept that this was possibly true for me now too. I had set out to travel for the rest of 2019 but didn't even last two months. So yes, it was technically true that I had failed. *And* I also know that an important part of the adventurous mindset is to remember that you can fail at something the first time, but that doesn't mean you can never go back and finish what you started. Yes/and—both of these things can be true. But that still doesn't mean it feels okay in the moment.

Making the decision to stop doing the thing you set out to do isn't where the hard part ends. When you turn around, you're going to find yourself face-to-face with feelings of failure and shame. There's so much excitement in the buildup. It's naturally going to be hard to come down—literally and figuratively. If you made an intentional decision, you should be able to confidently work through those feelings as they come up. It doesn't usually feel great, but you can still walk away knowing it was the right decision.

However, if you sabotaged the situation, it's a lot harder to process those thoughts and let go of the dreams you had. Quitting and going back to your old way of life is not going to be the easier choice to live with. Because once you've seen even a glimmer of what's possible for you, you will never forget it. The images of what could have happened if you'd kept going down this new path will pop up in your dreams and your daydreams. And the question "What if?" will consume your thoughts. So be really honest with yourself here. *Why are you stopping now? Why here? Is it possible to take a few more steps down the path and see what happens? Or does it feel like the right time to turn around?*

If you do decide to change your plans and walk away here,

you know it's going to be hard to process all your thoughts and feelings about it—and that's okay. Take all the time you need to do that work, and commit to doing it. It's important to name your feelings and work through them rather than push them down. What's going to come next can be even harder to handle: comments from the people who knew you were doing this—and who will find out that you stopped or failed or quit or turned around. Whatever you want to call it, you can be certain that they will have something to say. Sometimes they will try to reframe it for you, which is loving but not necessarily helpful. And sometimes they will just see it as a failure. As I wrote in my first book, "People will always make comments when you decide to live a countercultural lifestyle." They will have even more to say if you struggle with it.

Shame (On You)

I don't have a good analogy for how this next part directly relates to the outdoors because I've never experienced anything like this with my adventure partners. If someone has to stop and turn around, the whole group follows suit. No questions asked. Sure, you might feel a little disappointed that you didn't reach the summit. You were stoked to go and are sad to stop. But deep down, you also know that it was never really about the summit. It was about challenging yourself and spending time together in nature. So you wouldn't dare risk your friend's comfort or safety. It's not worth the pain and suffering, emotional or physical. If someone has to turn around, you know they feel even worse than you do — so you do whatever you can to make them feel supported. You support each other.

When my friend Pascal and I hiked Mount Finlayson in Victoria for the first time, she still had an intense fear of heights — specifically of being on an exposed path that left us open to a huge drop. Just minutes from the top, we rounded a corner and found ourselves extremely exposed, and she froze.

She tried to sit down and crab crawl along on all fours, but I went ahead and knew she'd have to stand and scramble up to get to the top eventually. She asked if we could stop there, and I just said yes. It didn't matter if we were ten minutes away or thirty seconds away. If she couldn't do it, we wouldn't do it — together. So we hiked back down and talked through her feelings because we both knew how hard it is to process the conflicting thoughts that come up when you have to change your plans.

I wish I could tell you this is what will happen when you're in the valley. I wish, more than anything, that I could tell you everyone in your life will support you through this part of your journey. Some people will! I don't want to paint a picture so dark that it scares you out of even attempting to opt out. Some people will understand that you're struggling, and they will say all the right things and try to help you find your footing again. But whether you quit early or you're just going through a period when you feel lost or uncertain, people know. They can sense it. And those people who tried to shame you out of changing paths to begin with will probably jump at this opportunity. As soon as they sense you have arrived here, be prepared for them to swoop right back in and chastise you for not succeeding on your first try.

The most obvious comments will be along the lines of *I told you so*. "I told you it would be hard." "I told you that would happen." "I told you that you couldn't do it."

Then they might list all the things you did wrong. "You didn't do enough research!" "You didn't plan or prepare properly!" "You did *that*?! Why would you do that?" "Oh, well that was a stupid decision!"

When you're lost and struggling to decide what to do, they

will even go so far as to remind you that "you wanted this." As though wanting to make a change means you're not allowed to feel lost, or "How dare you complain that it's not easy? Suck it up, buttercup. Deal with it. This is what you signed up for."

Sometimes these comments will hurt because you feel as though the people you love don't understand you. Or that they don't trust you to know what's right for you, let alone believe you can achieve something you set out to do. It's easy to feel as though they don't support you — and the reality with that one is that they don't, at least not in an unconditional way. When people choose to shame you for opting out, it's because they want you to live by their rules. Any attempt to choose a different path feels like a referendum on the one they have chosen, and nobody likes to feel attacked. They want you to stay in alignment with *their* goals and values, not to set out into the world and find your own. Because if you find a new way to live, they run the risk of having to see that their way isn't the only option — that maybe they aren't always right. They could even be telling you the stories that held them back from trying to live differently because they want you to do what they did. So they act out. They say things. They hurt your feelings. They try to reel you back in. And in the process, there is the potential that they will stop you from living the life you really want.

When you opt out for the first time, these words are going to be powerful. If you take these comments too close to heart, they can stop you from building up enough courage to even try in the first place. They can be part of the reason you self-sabotage and run home to the people you know and the path you were comfortable on before. They can leave you feeling misunderstood and alone. Worse yet, they can make you worry that they are right and everything they are saying is true.

When it feels as if someone can see inside you and pokes at every single one of your fears and insecurities, you will think it's because they know you. But all they know is that human beings walk this earth filled with fear. They have fears. And what they are doing right now is simply (albeit brutally) projecting their fears onto you. This is partially because they don't want you to force them to see that there is another way of living, but it's also a tactic to shame you into staying on their path with them. They know there is strength in numbers, and they don't want to lose any of the numbers on their side. So they will be quick to point out the things that they themselves are afraid of because they know you are probably afraid of them too. And then you will feel seen and understood and begin to worry that they are right. Before you even opted out, you *had* worried that you might not have done enough to prepare for it. Or that you *were* taking on too big of a risk. And you *definitely* worried that you would fail. And then you walk away from these interactions with people thinking, *Maybe they are right. Maybe I can't do this.*

It can take a long time to understand what's happening during this part of the journey. You might even have to opt out of a few different things, and experience this stage a few times for yourself, before you can see it as it's unfolding. If you do find yourself spiraling with self-doubt and shame, I want you to remember two things. The first is that nobody knows you better than you know yourself. Nobody, nobody, nobody. I mean nobody. It can feel as though people are reading your mind, but they're not. It's easy for people to offer input and suggestions. But at the end of the day, only you know what is right for you.

The second thing I want you to keep in mind is that this is how shame works. The goal is to make you feel ashamed. And you can feel ashamed only if you feel there might be some truth in it, only if you believe there is a reason you should feel guilty or embarrassed. So people will say things to make you feel guilty or embarrassed. I'm going to argue that you probably don't have any reason to feel like that about your opt-out. Are you a decent human being? Who was only trying to do something that felt right for you, and not hurt people in the process? I thought so! And that means you have absolutely nothing to be ashamed of.

These questions and comments are frustrating and can be condescending and sometimes downright hurtful. But the hard truth is, they're usually par for the course if you're living your life on your own terms. I'm not saying it's right, and it's definitely not fair. I just want you to be prepared for them. It can be hard to return to a place that wants you to stay the same. People will always make comments when you decide to live differently, and even more comments when you get lost or you fail at trying to live differently. You can't control what they say. But you can control how you react.

Talk It Through

I don't have a lot of friends who live the way I do. In fact, I don't think I have *anyone* I can call to confirm that being a sober, vegetarian, nomadic writer is actually going to work out for me. In the first chapter of her book *Braving the Wilderness,* Brené Brown perfectly expressed the same concerns about her work and career. She wrote, "There's no one ahead of me saying, 'It's okay. There are lots of professor-researcher-storyteller-leadership-entrepreneur-faithful-cussers out here. Here's the blueprint.'" At the end of every interview for her podcast, Fiona asks her guests what the hardest part of living another way is, and the answer is always along the same lines: "I don't know what I'm doing, and I have no one to talk to about it."

It's hard enough to talk about something while you're going through it. To make sense of what's happening when you're living in the messy middle. This is one of the many reasons I stopped writing my blog in 2018, and why I didn't share much about my first year of travel in any kind of public forum. Because everything felt uncertain. I've found a way to be com-

fortable living in that state of mind myself, but it's still difficult to talk and write about. To say you know what you're
doing for only the next week or month or three months, and
after that you'll just "see." To be open to letting things unfold
and trusting that you can handle any scenario you find yourself in. It's even harder when you try to talk about it and it
feels as though the person you open up to doesn't understand —
or worse, doesn't seem to support your choice.

If you find yourself in this situation with someone, you have
two choices: you can stop talking to the person and eventually
cut them out of your life, or you can try to have more open and
honest conversations and hope you can create a more intentional relationship in the process.

I can see why you might be tempted to stop talking to
someone who doesn't seem to understand or support you. I
really can. It's a behavior I grew up witnessing, so I unfortunately have a lot of experience practicing it myself. I know it's
hard to feel misunderstood and to feel judged. It's exhausting
to feel as though you have to explain yourself all the time. And
when you're doing something that you know is right for you,
despite the fact that you knew it would be hard, it already
feels as though it's you against the world sometimes. So I can
see why you wouldn't want to talk to the naysayers. You don't
need any additional discouragement!

Some writers might step in here and suggest that your next
move should be to immediately create boundaries between
you and these people. Trust me: I am all for boundaries —
especially after decades of being a people pleaser. But I'm
worried that the definition of the word "boundaries" has been
incorrectly translated by memes and pretty quotes we can
share on the internet. Most of what I see online inadvertently

directs us to put up walls and push people away. It has confused the idea of creating boundaries with shutting everyone out. Again, this is why I don't like all the little sayings thrown around that give overly simplistic solutions to complicated problems. Are there a few people you might have to cut out? Yes. People who are abusive or manipulative? Say goodbye to them! And you certainly don't need the ones who feel they can control you. So please, let them go. But if someone simply doesn't seem to understand you: cutting them out shouldn't be the go-to response. It's defensive and harmful for both of you.

If you choose to take the defensive route, be ready for the relationship to potentially end rather quickly. If the person you're going up against is defensive about their choices and you are defensive about yours, nobody will win. It will be two egos going head-to-head and both of you will lose, walking away with nothing more than some confusion and heartache. Also, if you act defensive, it will seem as though you have something to be defensive about. Do you? I don't think so! All you're doing is making a different lifestyle choice. So you don't need to get defensive. It's your ego trying to protect you, but you don't have to react this way.

Also, if you put too many walls around you, my fear isn't just that you will be alone. You are already alone, in a way, and you're figuring that out. I actually hope you get comfortable with being alone, for the mere fact that it's an important life skill to have—and one that helps you listen to and trust yourself better. My fear is that if you put too many walls up, you will make a lot of assumptions about how people might have reacted to your honesty. And if you make assumptions and you cut people off too soon, I'm afraid you might miss out on what could have been a really meaningful conversation — and relationship.

Can I suggest another way?

Instead of cutting people off, what if you tried to talk through the issue? I don't mean for that to sound quite so simple. It's a lot easier for me to type those words than it is to act on them, and acting on them is something I've only slowly gotten better at in recent years. But if someone doesn't understand you, what if you tried to clarify? Or if they made a comment that hurt you, what if you tried telling them that? And then what if you tried telling them how to fix it? Or how to be more supportive? What's stopping you? I can't speak for you, but I know what used to stop me.

I used to be too afraid to explain who I really was because I assumed people wouldn't like me. I didn't think I was good enough or smart enough or interesting enough. I just didn't think I was enough of anything. So if it seemed as if someone misunderstood me, I tried to ignore it. If they liked this "other" version of myself, sadly, I didn't want to risk showing them who I really was for fear that they might not like that version — the real version. Often, this meant I just went along with things, all because I assumed that people wouldn't like me. I was afraid to speak up for myself for the very same reasons. And I was really afraid to be needy. Some of these things were passed down to me, and some are things girls are conditioned to believe. What I can tell you now is that it all resulted in pain and confusion. I was hurt. Then I hurt people by cutting them off. And nobody knew what really happened.

The hardest thing I have to say next is that it's not entirely the other person's fault. It would be so much easier if we could point a finger and blame the person who didn't understand us, but it takes two people to communicate. A lot of us are hurting in our friendships and relationships because people cross our boundaries or don't meet our needs in some way. But most of the time, we don't tell people what we need. We just expect them to know, or to understand we are on a journey. Not only is it unfair to place an unspoken expectation on someone; it's also unfair to assume that people will always understand what we are doing and why. People can see only as far for you as they see for themselves. So we have to remember that if people aren't doing the same thing as us, they won't automatically understand. However, I don't always think that's for lack of wanting to.

I genuinely believe that the people who love you want to support you. They also want to be able to talk to you. Maybe they won't say the right thing at first, but they probably wish they could. I can't imagine that your loved ones are sitting around thinking up ways that they can intentionally hurt your feelings. If anything, my guess is that they are sad that you are going off in a new direction and potentially leaving them behind. They don't want the relationship to end, the same way you probably don't want it to end either. The only assumption we should make, then, is that everybody is doing the best they can with what they have.

Instead of getting angry or feeling sad or hurt by people, there's an opportunity to educate them. To tell them what you are doing and why. To teach them how to listen and how to love you. To ask for specific feedback or to tell them you aren't open to feedback at all. These are all aspects of creating an intentional relationship with someone—friendship or otherwise. On this topic, one of the best things my friend Azalea ever taught me is that you are 100 percent responsible for your own needs. That doesn't mean you have to walk through the world without friends or people to support you. It means you have to tell people who you are, how you are feeling, and what you need from them. And remember that if you don't ask, the answer is always no.

Azalea has been learning this lesson and putting it into practice since she was just nineteen years old. That's the age she was when she opened up her first relationship—and she's had mostly nontraditional relationships ever since. On top of learning how important it is to ask for what you need, Azalea has taught me it's equally important to take responsibility for the impact you have on others. That if you intended to communicate one thing and the impact isn't what you had intended, you need to clean it up. It's not about who is right or wrong. It's an opportunity to see where the breakdown happened, and for both of you to learn how to communicate in such a way that you can reach your intended outcomes. (Also, as a reminder to myself: cutting people off typically leaves a negative impact on both people. There's not much healing that can be done from that.)

It's okay if you don't do any of this stuff perfectly. Actually, let me be clear that you will *not* do it perfectly. It will get messy, you will unintentionally hurt each other's feelings, and you will both need to do the work to clean that up. Give yourself some grace, and then extend it to the people you share your truth with. It's scary to admit that you don't know exactly what you're doing—neither of you knows what they are doing in this situation. But if you take your wall down, maybe they will too.

When I first got back from the UK, I was struggling so much that I barely even told anyone I was home. I told my dad and my sister, as well as Emma and my girlfriends in Squamish. But I didn't tell anyone else. I didn't know how to communicate all the mixed emotions I was feeling, and I also didn't think I could handle any negative feedback about my failed adventure. When I finally started to share the news, no one was particularly unsupportive about my decision to come home early. However, some people made assumptions—and those hurt in their own way. Some people assumed my mental health must have taken a dive. Some assumed that something was wrong—with me or with someone in my family. Some decided I must be done with traveling and was ready to finally move back to my hometown. And some people even made assumptions about what other people might be thinking. They literally said that, if they were in my shoes, they would be worried about what other people would be thinking, and then they listed all the possible gossip that people could be coming up with. Do you know what that really means? *That they were the person making those assumptions about me!*

I could have been hurt. I was a little. And I could have gotten angry. But I now know that it's better to be compassionate instead. To understand that people make comments based on the information they have. If I don't give them all the information, I can't expect them to fully understand what I'm going through. And it's my job to tell them what I need.

To the people I cared about who made assumptions, here was my response: *It was a hard decision. I don't feel great about it right now. I have a lot on my mind, and I'm trying to work through what happened and what my options are. I don't really want to talk about it, but I appreciate you for thinking of me, and I'll come to you if I need any advice. Love you!* That's it. Message sent. And message received on their end.

If people don't respond appropriately? Try again. And if you're really not getting through and they keep hurting you? Well, maybe put the conversation on the back burner for a little bit. These are the moments when it's okay to create new boundaries. Your boundaries don't have to look like walls. My therapist once told me that she liked to think of boundaries as circles—little destinations you can point to and say to someone in your life, "Meet me here." Maybe you don't discuss certain topics in one circle with a particular friend, but it's safe to discuss these topics in another circle with another friend. There's a circle for everyone! I love this idea. It means you don't have to cut anyone off just because they aren't getting it perfectly right. You are allowed to simply change the shape of the relationship. That's intentional too.

So if you're stuck in the valley for some reason and aren't yet sure what the next right step is, please don't close yourself off. If you really want to lead by example, the best thing you can do is change the conversation by being open and honest about what you're trying to do. If you want to move forward, you have to forgive yourself for whatever has gone wrong so far. That's the only way to beat your own personal shame. And if you want to move forward in your relationships with people who might have said the wrong thing, you have to forgive them too—and give them the opportunity to support you the way I think you know they want to. They just might need a little assistance. Don't we all.

Take Care

I think it's safe for me to assume that you can now see why the valley is often the most difficult portion of a hike to navigate. Whether you've lost your sense of direction, you're looking up and around at all your seemingly impossible options, or you decide to stop and turn around here, it's tough. It's also tough if you've hurt yourself or even been hurt by others. This is the place where you have to make some big decisions. What you've been doing so far has been the beginning of a shedding process: letting go of a part of yourself that doesn't feel right anymore, and trying a new idea you have about yourself on for size. It is uncomfortable and confusing and demanding at times. This is painful work. In our interview, Gale described the entire process as tearing a muscle to make it stronger. With that analogy, you can see why this is the place where you need to take good care of yourself.

What does your body need? is another one of those simple but meaningful questions Azalea asks me whenever I reach out to her for help. I called her a few times throughout 2019, when I couldn't see what my next step was. And while you would think I could just ask myself that question by now, there's something about the way Azalea says it that helps me feel how important it is to listen to my body and find the answer. What my body needed after I returned home from the UK in May was space and silence. Time to be alone with my thoughts. It felt like a luxury, but also a requirement. It sometimes takes only one flight and a few hours to reach your physical destination, but it can take a lot longer to feel grounded there. And I certainly did not feel grounded after I returned from my failed attempt to travel all year.

Jet lag always leaves me feeling as though I'm stuck in two different places. As though my body is physically in the new time zone but my mind was left behind and is trying to catch up. People will tell you to try to stay awake and sleep only during "normal" hours in order to trick your mind to catch up quickly, but this never works for me. I still do that! I stay awake and try to sleep from, say, 10 p.m. to 6 a.m. But whenever I come back west from a trip, I have a really hard time adjusting. Instead of 6 a.m., I always find myself waking up between 3 a.m. and 4 a.m., and it typically takes two weeks before that rights itself and I begin to feel like myself again.

Along with having jet lag, I was also still dealing with some grief that comes with not being able to do what you really wanted to. In the past, I would have tried to numb this pain. To drink or eat or shop away my feelings. But I have learned the hard way not to do that. Over time, I have learned how to sit in the discomfort and feel my feelings. And I would rather feel the earth beneath my feet than numb myself from the human experience now. So I gave myself permission to take some time off, the way a thru-hiker might take a "zero" day or rest day. I needed to relax and come back into my body. In coming home, I knew there was no better place to do that than at my favorite secret spot in Victoria.

I'm certain there are secret spots in every town or city. Places that only the locals know about and like to keep that way. You might even have some in your neighborhood. But when you grow up on an island, you have access to a lot of secret spots—typically by the ocean—and keeping them a secret is part of the culture. I have a range of mixed feelings about this. The socially accepted answer for why you wouldn't want a place to get "busy" is because you don't want the land to be impacted by heavier foot traffic. And that's true. But the answer that's less acceptable to say, or admit to, is that a secret spot often feels like a place that belongs to you, and you want to keep it for yourself. You want it to stay quiet so you can continue to enjoy it. And that's true too. There's an entitlement to it, but it's a hard feeling and thought process to let go of, especially when it's something you were raised to believe. I know I constantly struggle with whether or not to tell people about my favorite place to go. For now, what I do believe is that if you take care of your secret spot, it will take care of you. We definitely took care of each other in May 2019.

After I returned home, I began every day doing the exact same thing: reading at my secret spot. As soon as I woke up, I would grab my book and my travel coffee mug and depart on my little adventure. To get there, you hike along a short trail that leads up and over some rocks and to a wooden bench that overlooks the ocean. Before I started reading, I would lie back on the bench, stretch my arms over and above my head, and feel the morning sun on my face. Sometimes I would study the color of the sky and think about how it might look different from the day before. Other times I would watch the clouds move and change shape. And every day I listened.

At first I heard only the most obvious noises. Wind blowing the tree branches. Birds chirping. A boat speeding by. As the days went on and I settled into this spot and myself again, I noticed how many more details I could hear. The sound of the wind whistling across my ear. Weightless birds landing on the ground and hopping around behind me. And kayakers talking on the water a few hundred feet below. It was as if the slower I moved, the more my eyes and ears opened to what was happening in the world around me.

Before I left my secret spot each day, I walked around to pick up any garbage or cigarette butts other people had left behind, and I threw it all out on my way home. My blogging friend David had once shared with me the advice that "when you don't know what to do, help someone else." I didn't know what I was going to do next, but I knew I could do this much while I was there. For three weeks, this was my morning routine. And I watched a lot of things change in that short time. The spring blooms came and went. Green grass started to brown. Trees went from being lush to looking as though they were begging for water. The season shifted. I shifted. I took care of my secret spot, and it took care of me. My mind caught up to me in the new time zone, and these little actions helped me feel more like myself. It was exactly what my body needed.

I once read a simple explanation of the four signs to look for when it comes to taking care of our basic needs. Hunger tells us we need to eat. Thirst tells us we need to drink water. Pain tells us we might be physically pushing ourselves too much and/or potentially hurting our bodies. And loneliness tells us we need social connection. In the valley, you could experience any and all of those things. So sit down. Eat one of the snacks you packed. Drink some water. Talk to your adventure partner or call a trusted friend. Take off your shoes to massage your feet. And stretch. Oh my gosh, please stretch. Do it right now, while you're reading this book! Stretching is the thing so many of us forget to do, or think we don't need to do, but then we pay the price when our muscles start to seize up on us later. The list of the benefits of stretching is long, but my favorite one to remember is that it helps me stay flexible: for a hike or for an adventure in opting out.

Take as long as you need here. There's no rush. That's one of the most beautiful things about doing this on your own: you get to decide how much time you need to work through each part of this process. When you feel ready to stand back up and carry on, you'll have a clearer mind and be better able to figure out what your next step is.

Your Senses

One of the only people I have ever gotten lost with is David. It was the fall of 2014, and he had come to Vancouver to visit a friend. Up until that point, we had only ever communicated through the comments sections of our blogs and via email. When he told me he was coming to the city, I offered to drive out from Port Moody and take him on a little hike in North Vancouver. After I picked him up, I plugged the name of the trailhead into one of the map apps on my smartphone and off we went.

We now live in a time when it's almost impossible to get physically lost in cities, thanks to the phones we carry with us. As long as we can pick up a signal from a nearby cell tower, these miniature handheld GPS devices can map out the fastest or most efficient routes for us to take from point A to point B. They also have the ability to reroute us if we miss a turn somewhere along the way. While I've obviously been grateful for this at times, I sometimes wonder if the map apps have taken away our ability to pay attention and navigate the world via our senses. Instead of taking in our surroundings, we rely on our phones to tell us exactly what to do, step by step. And if the maps don't have a route or take us in the wrong direction, it can literally stop us in our tracks. That's how David and I found ourselves at a dead end, still three miles away from our destination.

Feeling as though I should have known better or been a better leader for this little adventure of ours, I was mortified. But David, calm and cool as he always is, just sat back in my car and smiled. "I love getting lost," he said. "Then I will always know how to get there." What he meant in the moment was that I, as the driver, would probably never make the same mistake twice. If I looked at the road and paid attention to the route, from this moment on I would always remember how to get to this hiking trailhead. I just had to use my senses.

The reason I have memorized so many of the little comments David has made over the years isn't just because he seems to naturally speak in the language of greeting card quotes. It's also because his comments can always be applied to more than one situation. In 2019, I could see that losing sight of my path and deciding to change my travel plans wasn't a failure after all. And I couldn't look at it that way. The reality is that I was never going to do it perfectly. I knew that before I got started but had somehow forgotten, so I had to keep telling myself that now. Getting lost, therefore, was almost a gift. It showed me that I wasn't actually on the right path, and it helped me figure out what long-term travel needed to look like for me. Because I did want to keep traveling. I just had to do it differently. I had to think of a *new*, new path I could take.

After settling in at home, I started thinking about where I might have taken a wrong turn and gotten lost on this adventure. I had originally left for the UK without a clear idea of what I was doing. I had a list of places I might go, but nothing booked or penciled in past the first month. And while I wanted to be the kind of person who could be that spontaneous, I learned that I can't. Not only because I don't have a bottom-less budget, but also because my mental health can't handle it. It's also just not very fun to spend all your time in another country sitting in front of a computer and trying to find places to stay! The other lesson I learned, of course, was that I was no longer comfortable with taking many flights in a year. A few, sure—but not as many as I had once been comfortable taking or had thought I would take in the future. So my *new, new* path for long-term travel would require me to plan a little farther ahead and be smarter about my choices so the whole thing was more in line with my values.

Joseph Campbell wrote, "If you can see your path laid out in front of you, step by step, you know it's not your path. Your own path you make with every step you take. That's why it's your path." What I learned at the beginning of my long-term travel adventure, though, is that even if you're creating your own path, you can still get lost if you're not paying attention. If you're not asking yourself if it's where you want to be going. If you just blindly follow it, assuming you'll be happy with where you end up. And if you don't pay attention to the signs and whispers along the way that tell you otherwise. If you get lost, you can change your plans, but you don't have to change your goal. My goal was the same. I still wanted to spend the rest of 2019 in the UK. I would just see a little less of it, pick only one or two cities that felt right for me, and move at my own pace.

I spent the next few months doing more planning than I had ever done for a trip before. To start, I didn't book the long-term stays. Instead, I booked two shorter trips and decided to use them as sort of landmarks or trail markers—things to look forward to, and also to help me plan the first section of my time around. The first was a retreat that Nicole was hosting out in the Suffolk countryside. That would take place in the first week of August, so I booked my flight to London for then. The second thing I booked was a trip to Scotland with a friend from the U.S. We would meet in London and take the train up to Edinburgh at the end of September. That left me with six weeks in between. I didn't know where I wanted to spend them yet, but I knew it had to be in just one city.

Rather than be disappointed with being home, I took full advantage of summer in BC. I hiked often, celebrated my birthday in Squamish, and spent more time at my secret spot. I also went to a few documentary screenings with my friend Victoria, including one that looked at wild salmon's slide toward extinction and another on the circular economy. I learned more about what was happening in the province and started to figure out which causes might matter most to me. And then I committed to donating at least 1 percent of my income to environmental nonprofits and dreamt up ways I could give back to places I visited in the future. All this felt like a step in the right direction.

As the date of my flight to London grew nearer, I got a surprise email from a longtime reader of my blog and newsletter. In it, she shared that she knew of an Airbnb in Cardiff, Wales, that might be the "perfect place to write." I looked at the Airbnb online, and it did look nice, but I hadn't even considered Cardiff before. I wanted to see Wales, yes, but hadn't known where to start. *Would I like Cardiff? Was it too big of a city for me? Would I make any friends in a university town?* I didn't know the answers to those questions. When I plugged my dates into the calendar on the Airbnb listing, though, the price was more than right. In fact, it was exactly what I had been hoping to spend when I was in the UK in the spring. I didn't know if I would like Cardiff, but I booked a six-week stay there anyway.

I can't look back at this experience and say I *loved* getting lost on this path of mine. I didn't love all the feelings that came up, and I didn't love trying to navigate my way through them and figure out what long-term travel needed to look like for me personally. So I don't quite share David's enthusiasm for getting lost. But he was right about one thing: getting lost taught me how to get where I really wanted to go. It helped me further expand my self-awareness, determine a new value, and come up with a plan that was right for me. I wouldn't make the same mistakes twice. So long as I paid attention, I would always remember how to travel my own way. I just had to use my senses.

SECTION 4

The Slope

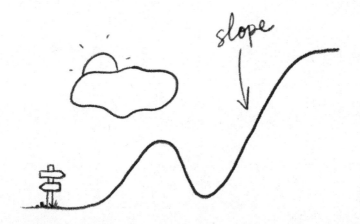

slope

The Slope

While there's no set amount of time you will be in the valley, as soon as you've finished navigating your way through it, you will find yourself staring up at the slope. Technically speaking, a slope is simply the side of a mountain. Some mountains have gentle slopes, which offer easy, gradual climbs. Other mountains have steep slopes, which might include sections you need to scramble up or might even require special equipment. Whenever I'm opting out, the slope typically looks steep but has what are known as switchbacks: a path that zigzags back and forth with hairpin turns. Switchbacks are carved out to help a steep climb feel more gradual, but it can take a lot of motivational pep talks to complete them—and get yourself up to the summit.

What makes this final ascent more manageable is that you've essentially been training for it throughout the process of opting out. Your first ascent up to the viewpoint taught you how to slowly ease into the journey rather than try to take on too much and hurt yourself—or hurt your chances of staying on this new path. It also taught you how to embrace an adventurous mindset, follow your curiosity, and walk through life with a new sense of wonder. You discovered you don't have to complete a perfect opt-out because there is no perfect way to change paths in life. The whole thing can simply be a learning experience.

Following that, the important (albeit uncomfortable) downhill hike and work you did in the valley stretched your muscles and built up your strength and resilience. You might have stumbled a little bit, or lost your way, and even forgotten what you were doing and why. You might have also struggled to

159

communicate with some of the people in your life, or started to feel as though you were losing them. None of this was easy. But the valley is also where you paused so you could avoid spiraling, and it reminded you of what you're working toward. You might have changed direction slightly or rerouted altogether. But in the end, you self-guided your way through the challenges, and now you're here.

While everything you've done so far might be both beautiful and painful to look back on, I would encourage you to keep the lessons you've learned in your back pocket right now. You will need quick access to them while you're hiking up the slope. That's not to say the slope is going to be equally painful, because it won't be. If anything, I like to think of the slope as the period of time when you get to set your own pace and finally see what life can be like when you're on this new path. It's the time to settle in and enjoy yourself.

This part of your opt-out will still come with questions and challenges. The higher you climb, the farther you will walk away from everyone who confronted you in the valley. Unless they've decided to join you, you're going to put more distance between you and anyone who didn't fully support you—and you will feel it. The good news is that, if you're open to it, you're going to cross paths with some incredible new people on the slope. You will also continue to build upon existing friendships and relationships with people who might not have been front and center before. People who understand what you're trying to do, and who will hold out their hands to help you get where you want to go.

It's safe to say that the slope will likely be the longest section of your adventure up to the summit. But don't let that scare you, because this is also one of the most rewarding sections. The slope is where you are piecing together everything you know you want. But it also requires letting go of some things you don't want along the way. For that reason, you will need to be on the slope until this new path you've chosen becomes a way of life — and that could take a while.

As an example, after working through some issues in the valley of my sobriety, I was on the slope for another three-plus years before I felt as though my sobriety was fully integrated into my life. With self-employment, I had two years of ups and downs before I eventually found my slope, and it took another eighteen months or so to reach the summit after that. For both opt-outs, these were the months and years when I was finding my rhythm, when decision-making slowly became easier and easier, when letting go of people and their expectations of me became less painful, and when I finally and unapologetically let myself have and feel what I wanted. They were challenging climbs, but I wanted to do them.

From what I've seen, the people who make it up the slope are those who are ready to let go of their past selves, and who are fully willing to stand out (and perhaps stand alone) on their journeys. After working through their initial anxiety or fear about what they might be getting themselves into, the people who make it up the slope know exactly what they are leaving behind, and they are confident it's the right choice now. As soon as you feel ready for that, take that next first step up. You can do this.

Hike Your Own Hike

"Hike your own hike" is a prevalent phrase used among thru-hikers—people who complete long-distance hikes from one starting point to another. The meaning has gotten a bit muddled, and in some cases is now used to tell hikers they aren't hiking the "right" way, as though there is such a thing. Imagine sharing your plans with someone and getting a sarcastic "Okay, hike your own hike, then. Good luck with that!" in return. That was not the original intention for the phrase, and it's not the one I want us to use when we hear the stories of other people who are opting out and changing paths in life. For us, "Hike your own hike" means only one thing: "I'm so glad you are actively and intentionally creating the life you want, not following or copying anyone else's. Hike your own hike, my friend!"

When you begin your climb out of the valley, you should have a sense of clarity that leaves you feeling both calm and equipped. Equipped to make everyday decisions, and calm enough to take at least the next few steps in front of you and see what happens. With opting out, I have found that after stumbling through the valley, I always exit feeling as though I have finally committed to whatever change I had originally set out to make. I may still have some hurt feelings or a few wounds to lick. And I will still find myself in situations that would normally trigger me. But I've dealt with the situations that forced me to ask myself the really tough questions—and now I'm ready to live out my choices. Not the choices that anyone else has made for me, or that I see others making for themselves. This is the time to set my own pace, and create the life and routine I want on this new path of mine.

"Routine" doesn't need to be anywhere near as strict as it sounds. When I wanted to stop working so much and finally start being the person who spends more time outside with her friends, blocking off Tuesday on the calendar set the intention. Occasionally, there were weeks when Pascal or I couldn't meet up for Adventure Tuesday, but we never took it off the calendar. One week off didn't mean the whole thing was off. It was still a commitment, not to each other but to ourselves. We always wanted to have an adventure to look forward to, so we kept it penciled in.

Sometimes the new "routine" isn't a routine at all. Sometimes it has nothing to do with your daily life, and is instead about how you cope with life. A few years into my sobriety, after I had gotten through things like a breakup and my parents' divorce without drinking, I finally climbed out of the valley, knowing I didn't need alcohol as a coping mechanism anymore. I was equipped with new tools—deeper self-awareness, knowledge that I could reach out to certain friends, and trust that I could feel my feelings and survive—and I used, and continue to use, those tools whenever tough situations come up.

Hiking your own hike can mean finally knowing what dietary choices are right for you and making them every day. Or getting into a groove with your business, and knowing what kind of work you are willing to take on and what kind of work you should turn down. Hiking your own hike is no longer thinking about how to make someone comfortable with your new choices. It's knowing what works for you, and what doesn't work for you, and not being afraid to communicate that with anyone.

With long-term travel, however, hiking my own hike actually had everything to do with routine. Now that I knew I couldn't be as spontaneous as some of my friends, or as spur-of-the-moment as the people whose travel I read about or followed online seemed to be, I knew that routine would be the key to living and traveling the way I wanted to.

When I shared my decision to go back to the UK and spend at least six weeks in Cardiff, not surprisingly, I received mixed responses. Emma was enthusiastic and excited for me, as she always is. My family actually liked the idea because Wales is the country my dad's parents had retired to and passed away in (albeit up north). And some friends thought Cardiff sounded nice. But most of them wondered what I was going to do there—and in one place—for so long. "Work!" was my reply. "Just live and work." The first draft of this book was due in December, so nobody argued with that, but going to another country just to live and work was still a foreign concept to them. It was to me too! I didn't know what temporarily setting up life in another country looked like, and I didn't know if I would like it there. But I did have a home base—and I knew now that was the most important piece of this puzzle.

I flew to London in early August and took the train out to

Ipswich. At the train station, I met the three other women who had signed up for the retreat Nicole was hosting in the Suffolk countryside. I had never gone on any kind of retreat before and naturally had some anxiety about entering the unknown. But the few days we spent together turned out to be a gift, and ultimately helped me ease into life in the UK.

We started every day with a slow morning, which has been a practice of mine since I first did a thirty-day slow morning experiment in 2017. For me, slow mornings start by not rushing to get out of bed. I'll stretch a little, look at my phone (not going to lie about this), and get up when I feel ready. Then I make coffee and breakfast and either read a book for a few minutes or start listening to a podcast. Sometimes slow mornings last for fifteen minutes; sometimes they last for an hour. We had about an hour before we dove into the work we were doing at the retreat.

With Nicole's guidance, we spent our days doing self-reflection and personal goal-setting exercises. In the late afternoons, a guest joined us, and we cozied up in the living room for an informal interview/chat facilitated by Nicole. One of the guests was my friend and an author whose work I love, Laura Jane Williams. Laura is someone who has opted out of many things, whether she realizes it or not. At the time of writing this, her most recent opt-out was actually two opt-outs wrapped into one: (1) she left London and moved out to the country, closer to her parents, so she could eventually (2) start the adoption process and become a mother on her own terms but with a good support system close by. Laura made the first decision knowing that the second one would take time. We had discussed it over brunch the first time we met, in June 2018, and shed a few tears over our eggs. The kind of tears that come out only when you can feel how meaningful a choice is for someone. It was now more than a year later, and the journey had come with peaks and valleys, as most opt-outs do. But Laura had followed her heart, and I still felt her strength in my own.

I left the retreat three days later with three new friends from three different countries (the UK, USA, and Sweden) and three new personal goals to focus on. From Ipswich I took the train back to London, then took the London Underground to a different station, and then took another train to Cardiff. The moment I arrived and stepped out onto the platform, I was greeted with warmth. August weather in Cardiff was similar to what I would have been experiencing in Victoria: temperatures hovering around 75 degrees Fahrenheit (24 degrees Celsius), some humidity, and a light breeze if you're by the water. I felt an even greater warmth when I checked into my Airbnb near Cardiff Bay and was greeted by my host. The Airbnb was her friend's home when the woman wasn't working overseas, and you could see it in the details. The deep couch that looked as though it was made for you to sink into and read a book on. Lights in all the right corners. The fully equipped kitchen. And extras of everything you might need, including bedding, towels, and toiletries. It was comfortable, set up in such a way that you could quickly unpack and feel settled. When I had booked this place, I didn't know what to expect. It just looked like a nice flat and was the right price. Standing in the living room, with the balcony door open and the fresh air flowing through, I knew I was home.

Before I left Victoria, I wrote down the four things that made up the majority of my routine so I could try to re-create it in any city I went to. Aside from a home base, I wanted a coffee shop, a grocery store, a trail (to walk or hike), and access to something big in the wild that gave me perspective (such as a mountain or body of water). A friend had told me about a coffee shop in the city that he thought I might like, and I found a few grocery stores in between there and my flat. And it took only a few days of exploring on foot to find a couple of quiet trails, in parks and along the water. Once I had these sorted out, I started my days as I would have if I was working on any big project at home. I woke up, slowly walked 1.5 miles to the coffee shop, and worked all morning. Then I walked home, maybe picked up some groceries along the way, and took a couple of hours off to walk or run by the water. I also took at least one day off each week so I could leave Cardiff and go on an outdoor adventure in another part of Wales, and sometimes I took a second day off to meet up with a friend in another city.

This wasn't the travel story I'd seen other people share before, and it didn't feel like one that would be particularly interesting to share in these pages. But this is what I had wanted when I first decided to attempt to travel full-time. The routine supported my work, and it especially supported my mental health. It was also the thing that made the whole journey finally feel less challenging. By doing what was right for me, I could now properly enjoy it. I still didn't know if I would love Cardiff, but I knew this way of living wasn't about reaching a particular outcome. It was about experiencing life in different countries, and this was one I had chosen for myself. Experience over outcome, always.

There is no one right way to travel, the same way there is no one right way to live, and especially no one right way to hike. So I have come to realize that "Hike your own hike" means there is really no one right way to do any of this. It means listen to your body and do what is right for you, every single day. It is an act of self-awareness and confidence. It is also an act of self-love. If we use this phrase in the world of opting out, may it be used as a rally cry or a blessing we give to others who are trying to fully integrate their choices into their lives. Of course, it should also be used as one of the many pep talks we will have to give ourselves.

Switchbacks

I briefly described what switchbacks are in the introduction to this section, but let me try to better explain them here. Imagine taking a piece of paper and a pencil and drawing a zigzag line from the bottom to the top. Start at one of the bottom corners, draw a line to just above the bottom corner on the other side, and then keep repeating that, slowly taking your lines higher and higher as you go. Back and forth, back and forth, each line a little bit shorter than the last and higher on the page. Now imagine taking that piece of paper and holding it up to a picture of a mountain. This is what a set of switchbacks looks like.

As I mentioned, switchbacks are carved out to help a steep climb up a slope feel more gradual. Rather than struggling the whole way or requiring special equipment to hike tougher terrains, they are meant to make the experience a bit more manageable. That sounds nice, and it's kind of others to create them for us. However, even though I know switchbacks technically make it easier on our bodies, they can also make the hike feel longer.

Switchbacks

When you're staring up at the face of a steep slope, you need motivation to even take the first step up. You know you want to get to the summit, but you also know it's going to take time and effort. So you push yourself to take the first step, and you start the climb. But after every line of a switchback, you look up and down the slope and realize you've barely moved — perhaps you've hiked up only another twenty or thirty vertical feet. At every hairpin turn, you stop and think, *Am I there yet?!* For a long time, the answer to that question is *Sorry, you're not even close.*

It can feel as though you're going nowhere for a long time, but I promise you are getting somewhere — with both your outdoor adventure and your adventure in opting out. You just need to be prepared for these moments. Instead of feeling as though I'm lost in despair in the valley, I find that switchbacks on the slope of an opt-out feel more like a conversation in my head. Rather than like emotional ups and downs, it's more as though your mind is wrestling side to side with two different stories: the old stories that subconsciously made many of your decisions in the past, and the newer, more conscious voice that is trying to speak up for who you are today. Maybe the old you would've quit here. Given up when you realized how long it would take. Or maybe it would've told you that you couldn't handle it. That you weren't equipped for the challenge. Back in the valley, you might have still listened to those scripts running through your head. You might have believed you couldn't do it and/or quit altogether. But if you're on the slope, you already know what feels right for you, and what you're capable of. You just need to keep telling yourself that here and reminding yourself what you're working toward.

So far I was loving my new routine in Cardiff. Slowly

getting to know the staff at Little Man, the coffee shop I worked out of most days. Spending sunny afternoons reading in Cathays Park behind City Hall and rainy afternoons curled up on the couch. But as I was nearing the end of my six weeks in Cardiff, I knew I needed to figure out where I was going to go. I had my trip to Scotland in September all mapped out, but that took me only up to October 1. After that, the world was my oyster again — or at least that's what the old story in my head was telling me. I started daydreaming about going to Austria or Germany, two countries that were high on my list before I gave up my condo in Squamish. Norway was also high on the list, as was all of Scandinavia, really. So I spent a few evenings online, scrolling through potential rentals in some of the cities on my bucket list. I also wanted to visit my cousin in Amsterdam and spend more time with friends in London, so I was looking at places in both of those cities too.

Fortunately, it didn't take me long to realize I wasn't getting anywhere with my searches. There were lots of options, but wanting to travel everywhere by train rather than plane and knowing how much longer that would take, plus knowing the time required to get set up in a new city again, made it all feel a bit more daunting — especially when I knew what my top priority was for the fall: finishing this book. The old story in my head about how I had the freedom to go anywhere and do anything I wanted wasn't serving me. It was a dream, a fantasy I used to have about who I thought I could be. But I couldn't actually be that kind of traveler, at least not right now. I had to make plans based on who I really was and what I had to do in this moment: I was a writer who needed a routine so she could get her work done.

After a few days of dreaming about all the places I could go, I decided to look at what was available in Cardiff for the fall. The flat I was currently living in was available for the month of November, so I booked that. Then I found a similar flat on the same street and booked that for the month of October. I thought I was set. I could go to Scotland and then come back and keep my exact same routine for two more months, minus having to move my bags a couple of times. This was perfect. I had told my new friends in Wales and had sent Emma pictures of the next flat I would be staying in. I was getting excited! And then the owner of the second flat canceled my October booking, claiming that the website hadn't charged me the full price. Was I willing to pay hundreds of dollars more? No, I was not. And with that, it was back to the drawing board.

I will spare you the boring details about how much time I spent after that looking for an affordable home. It took so long that I questioned whether or not I would find a place at all. I even wrestled with staying in Scotland for October and coming back in November, but that wasn't what I really wanted. I wanted to be in Cardiff. It had taken a few switchbacks, or a little back-and-forth in the decision-making process, but now I knew that's what I really wanted.

In the end, I booked a place from October 7 to November, when I could move back into the flat I loved. The second place was in a new neighborhood, so I would have to shift my routine slightly and I'd get to explore another part of the city. That felt good and supportive of my overall goal. But that still left me with a handful of days and nights at the start of October when I needed to find a place to stay. I didn't know where I would go yet, but that felt like a relatively easy challenge now that the rest was taken care of. I knew I would be able to figure it out before the time came.

Aside from this situation, I didn't have a lot of memorable switchbacks in Wales, or on my slope of long-term travel in 2019 in general. I don't think that's because there were none. I think it's because I was eventually so clear on what my intention was (to stay put and write) that it became a lot easier to make decisions that would support it. But I've had tougher slopes to climb with previous opt-outs.

With my sobriety, the switchbacks were all the situations that popped up where I wasn't sure how to show up as my full, honest self. Where I wasn't yet comfortable going to certain social events but didn't want to miss out on them either. Or where I didn't want someone to dislike me, or even judge me, if I told them I didn't drink, although I also knew I was never going to drink with them. I didn't go back on my sobriety then, and I never will now. But it took a long time for me to be certain that this was my decision for life, no matter what anyone else thought about it. My mind wrestled with a lot of switchbacks until it finally got to the point that I can *always* confidently say, "I don't drink!"

Not surprisingly, switchbacks are more of a mental challenge than a physical one. Your best chance at completing them is to know they are coming, because they *are* coming. In the early stages of a slope, you will probably find that it takes longer to make decisions because they feel bigger or more complex at the start. You might sit with a decision for days or even weeks as you actively try to change the story you're telling yourself about why you can't do it. But the farther along you go on your adventure in opting out, the more confident you will be in your choices, and the easier it will be to make them. Then with each decision you make, and every switch-back you hike, your zigzag line will get a little shorter and inch its way up as you get closer and closer to what you want. It's okay to stop at the turns to catch your breath and see how far you've come. Just don't stop altogether. You're really doing this now. You're getting closer to what you want.

Breathe

One thing to remember about hiking is that there will always be points where you start to feel as though you're out of breath. It doesn't matter how "fit" you are or how much experience you have. Even if you're moving at your own comfortable pace, your heart rate will still naturally go up with an incline. If you're on a mountain that has any kind of serious elevation (let's say ten thousand–plus feet above sea level), the air will become thinner the higher you go, making it physically harder to breathe. But let's assume your opt-out won't be taking you anywhere that high yet. You'll still feel better if you take a few breaks to catch your breath.

You might do this at the hairpin turn on your switchbacks where you're trying to make a decision. It might help you to stop and think about how you want to keep moving forward. It might give you some time to consider whether you're happy with the life you're making for yourself on this new path, or whether there's anything you'd like to shift. It might even help you spot things you couldn't see from farther down the slope and inspire you to carve out a little path off to the side so you can go explore what's over there for a bit. It could also simply leave you feeling reinvigorated and ready to carry on. It can serve many different purposes. No matter what, though, the break will give you a break from doing the work. Personally, the reason I love taking breaks on both hikes and opt-outs is because they give me an opportunity to have more fun.

We haven't really explored the topic of having fun yet. Up until this point, we have mostly looked at why you might want to opt out of something, how to begin, and some of the ups and downs you could face in doing so. Although I've showed you a few of the early benefits of opting out that you might experience at the start, this journey has probably felt like a lot of work with just a little bit of pleasure and self-care. But if you haven't already found yourself enjoying parts of the adventure, the slope is the place to change that.

It feels strange to say that I took a "break" from my new life in Wales. That wasn't the original intention of my trip to Scotland. For close to a year, my friend Kara Pérez and I had been talking about going on some kind of trip together. She was among the first few friends I had told I would be leaving Squamish and attempting to travel full-time, and she was also one of the friends who showed nothing but full support and enthusiasm. Kara knew I wanted to spend most of my time in the UK, and she had been invited to a wedding outside London in September 2019. "If you're still there, we should do something!" she said on a Skype call one day. "Maybe go on a hike or a trip or something?!" Of course my answer was yes.

In the months between my first failed attempt and my flight back to London in August, Kara and I returned to that conversation and came up with "just enough" of a plan. She would fly over from the U.S. for the wedding, and we would meet in

London afterward and take the train up to Edinburgh together. From there, we would rent a car (or "hire a car," as the Brits would say) and drive to the Isle of Skye. We had booked Airbnbs, reserved the car, and so on to make sure our basic necessities were taken care of. But our only plan for Skye was to go hiking every day. We would figure it all out once we got there.

In late September 2019, one year after our first conversation about going on a trip together, Kara and I found each other in London inside a crowded King's Cross station. It was the first time we had seen each other in person since the fall of 2017, when we had both attended a conference in Dallas, Texas. That's where we had first met—at the same conference the year before.

Kara and I had different backgrounds and lived different lives, but we had both publicly documented our debt repayment journeys online and became friends through that process. While I eventually stopped working in the personal finance space, Kara went on to start her own company, Bravely, so she could give a community of self-identified women the financial tools to bridge the gap between their dreams and their realities. She continues to be one of the most curious and passionate women I know in that space, and her enthusiasm is naturally contagious. We also shared very similar thoughts on how we wanted to incorporate travel into our lives. In 2016, we actually went on individual road trips through the U.S. at the same time, found each other at the conference in San Diego, and then met up again in Monterey, California. Seeing her again in the UK felt like coming home in its own way. As much as I was loving my life in Wales, I couldn't deny that it felt comforting to see a familiar face.

Our train ride up to Edinburgh was just shy of six hours

long. We spent the time catching up on everything from the past year as we looked out the window and watched nothing but green grass and countless sheep go by. We had a lovely night in Edinburgh and another in Inverness the next day. But the drive from Loch Ness over to Skye following our stop at Urquhart Castle ended up being one of the most memorable parts of the trip. The farther we drove into the Scottish Highlands, the more desolate they became. The landscape slowly switched from bright green trees and hills to mountains in muted tones of green, yellow, and even red and black. "Are we on Mars?!" was a question we asked over and over as we drove. And the scenes became only more dramatic after we crossed Skye Bridge.

For the next four days, Kara and I started our mornings with the same routine: we cooked breakfast, made coffee, and mapped out our day. This was often prompted by the question Azalea always asked me: *What would feel good for you today?* What felt good for us both was to go for a hike in the morning; maybe do a slow drive around a new part of Skye, with stops at random places along the way; and then come home in the mid- or late afternoon. Kara would do a little work, I would read and relax, and then we would cook dinner and watch a movie. We figured out our hike over breakfast, packed lunches and snacks, and left home with enough resources to get us through the day. Aside from the hike, there was no major goal. We didn't want to rush around constantly or try to cross a million things off any lists. We simply wanted to enjoy our time there, and that's what we did. Experiences over outcomes, always.

After Kara and I returned to Edinburgh and parted ways, I kept this same routine going for a few more days but in a new city: Paris. It turned out Chris and Mimi were there for her work and had an extra room at the apartment they were staying in. The dates lined up perfectly with when I needed to find a place to stay, so when the invitation to join them was extended, *hello,* I said yes to that too!

Altogether, I got a two-week break from work. Two weeks to spend time with friends and have deep and meaningful conversations. Two weeks to explore more of the world on foot. While I didn't exactly need a break from Wales, the time away helped me see that I was finally doing everything I had originally hoped to do: live somewhere new and occasionally travel to other parts of Europe when I could afford to. So maybe it wasn't a break after all. Maybe I was just living out my goals and values. Maybe I was doing exactly what I wanted and was simply stopping to make sure of it. Either way, it was an awe-inspiring time that reminded me of how far I had come, and it reinvigorated me to keep going down this new path of mine.

When you first start hiking, you might worry that taking a break will make you look bad. It doesn't. It helps you enjoy the overall experience more. The same is perhaps even more true for opting out. It's not a race. You don't need to prove anything to anyone, and it doesn't need to be a constant struggle. You have a choice about how to proceed, every step of the way. This is the place where you are intentionally creating the life you want, one that is ultimately aligned with your values. If you're doing that, it should naturally start to be more enjoyable. If you're not enjoying the new path you're taking, what's the point?

My suggestion: stop as often as you'd like. Look up and down and all around you to see how far you've come. Do some self-reflection and make sure this feels good. And before you carry on, take a deep breath. The kind of breath where you can feel the air move through your nose, fill up your lungs, puff out your chest, and give you the oxygen you need to take your next steps. Remember that the climb up the slope is long, and the summit isn't the only thing you should be working toward. You're allowed to enjoy the journey.

Adjust Your Straps

When I first started hiking, I always brought more stuff in my backpack than I would need. It's the same way we pack more clothes and toiletries than we could possibly use on a trip. It's not just that we don't seem to have a clear understanding of how much one human actually uses. We tell ourselves that we are happy to carry around a bit more stuff "just in case" we need it, or because we want to be ready for any of the catastrophic what-if situations we've dreamt up before leaving home. Essentially, we are afraid of entering the unknown, so we bring everything we have in an attempt to ease some of our fears.

At first you might not notice or mind how much extra stuff you're carrying. But the farther along you go, the more you can feel the added weight of it all—especially when you're on an incline. Your lower back starts to hurt, and you might find yourself changing your gait or posture to ease the pain. And if the backpack is really heavy, or if it isn't fitted properly, you will feel the straps start to dig into your shoulders and hips, even causing blisters or bruises. If you're out in nature, there's not much you can do in this situation. You'll have to carry it all out, and then go through your backpack and figure out what you didn't use and don't need to bring next time. But if you're opting out, you can slowly let things go when you're on the path.

Of course, not all opt-outs have physical objects, though I suppose you could overprepare for some and then realize you don't need certain things along the way. Instead, I would imagine that the heaviest things you've been carrying on this journey so far have been relationships. Specifically, some of the relationships you've been afraid to lose since the beginning. Since *before* the beginning. Relationships you were so afraid to lose you almost didn't even let yourself think about opting out. But the fear of losing people often leads to doing things you don't really want to do and to connecting in all the wrong ways, and that's not a way to live. If you are still carrying around relationships that are holding you back in some way, it's time to dig through your bag and see what you can let go of.

I'm going to be really honest and tell you this is a hard chapter for me to write. I know what it's like to be on both ends of this: to be the person who lets a relationship go, and to be the person who watches someone walk away from them. It's not easy to be in either position, and there's no specific formula for who to let go of or why or how. The healthiest and most loving thing I can do here is take the blame off the other person and model what that looks like in hopes that you can do it as well. We don't need to point fingers and shame anyone. In a way, it's not even fair. The truth is that you are the one who has walked away because you are the person who has changed. And the farther along you go on your journey, the more obvious that will become. Here's how this might show up for you.

- You might feel as though you don't have anything in common anymore.
- You might feel as though you have nothing to contribute to conversations.
- You might feel as though you can't relate to their experiences.
- You might feel as though you don't agree with their views.
- You might feel as though you aren't being supported.
- You might feel as though you have to make up for the fact that you're different now.
- You might feel as though you need to be a different or old version of yourself around them.
- You might feel as though you can no longer show up as your full self.
- You might feel as though they don't care.

Any or all of the feelings you are experiencing: they are valid. And if you're open to looking at it this way, I think it's safe to assume that the person you are in a relationship with is feeling the same way. Put yourself in their shoes and then go back and read those same bullet points. It's tough to think you might be making someone feel that way, right? But this is what happens, unintentionally, when we are afraid to let go of a relationship that isn't working. When we hold on to someone too tightly, out of fear, all we end up doing is trapping them— and ourselves—in a version of the relationship that doesn't serve either person anymore. Honestly, it doesn't even exist. As soon as we can recognize and accept that, we can begin to loosen our grip and let go.

I didn't lose any friends when I was traveling, but over the years I have had to let go of a lot of friendships and relationships. Some came to natural completion points, and others required a little more discussion. None of them were necessarily easy to navigate, and there is always some amount of grief to process. But there are a couple of things I can share with you that might help.

First, the anxiety or fear that you had about losing the relationship is almost always worse than the process of actually letting the person go. Anxiety and fear are tricky like that. They paint a lot of scary what-if pictures in your mind, which will make you hold on to people "just in case." But the reality is often not even close to what you imagined. It hasn't been for me. As an example, do you remember when I was scared to delete my Facebook account because my worst-case scenario was that I would lose touch with people? That's been true — *and* it hasn't impacted my life in any significant way. If I think of someone and really want to reconnect, I will just contact a couple of friends and see if they know how I can get in touch with that person. A slightly more painful example is the friends I lost after I quit drinking. But again, it was not as bad as I had imagined. The people who cared more about me than about whether or not I drank helped us navigate and change how we socialized. And the few people I lost sadly chose to prioritize their relationship with alcohol, which isn't about me at all. When you know it's not personal, it's easier to accept the reality and slowly let go.

Second, in case you need the reminder, you've already let go of a number of things in this process: family stories, expectations, and messages that told you who you should be and how you should live. And stories you used to tell yourself about who you thought you should be. You were scared to do

185

all that, but you started opting out anyway. Now you're getting closer to understanding what you want your life to look and feel like. And you've done some work here, so you already know how to deal with the ups and downs of it, which means you know how to handle this too.

I won't tell you exactly how to let a relationship go. That is going to look different for every single person you go through this with, because no two relationships are the same. Instead, I'd like to paint a different picture that might help you accept the situation and process the loss. This is something an old coworker shared with me when I lost a friend in my early twenties. The analogy isn't exactly environmentally friendly, but it still helps me to this day.

Imagine that everyone in your life is currently driving a car down the same road. Sometimes you'll drive next to everyone for a while. Sometimes people will need to go faster or slower, but you'll still be going in the same direction. And then, every so often, someone will take an exit. It might be someone you love; it might be you. But it's just a simple exit, and that's okay. Everyone is moving in the direction they need to go. You can wave goodbye and miss people, but it doesn't need to be dramatic. You can simply trust that you were on the same road together for a reason, and be grateful for the time you spent together.

While I haven't lost anyone because of my most recent opt-out, to move around and travel the way I do is to live in a constant practice of letting go. Saying goodbye to your home. Then saying goodbye to the places that become your home. Leaving behind the people who lived and loved you there. Walking away from the paths you stepped on, and the trees you touched, and the flowers you smelled, and the birds you watched and listened to. Knowing you may never see any of it again. Being grateful for the time you had. Then breaking your own heart a little bit more, with every step you take. And reminding yourself that all things end eventually, while trusting that you lived that experience for a reason.

So, the question that inspired this book: "Did you lose anyone along the way?" Yes, I have. And so will you. And so will everyone — whether you're opting out or not. If you are opting out, though, the most important lesson I pulled from Lori Gottlieb's book *Maybe You Should Talk to Someone* is that change travels with loss. It's the simplest equation, really. If you want to change your life, you have to change your life — and lose something, or perhaps someone, along the way. It's said that people come into your life for a reason, a season or a lifetime. Rather than fear it, maybe we could try to remember that our time together was always going to be temporary. So loosen your grip. Adjust your straps. Release whatever is still holding you back from walking through this world as your full self. And remember that a successful relationship doesn't have to be one that lasts forever. It can simply serve a purpose. I hope you can find some peace in the letting go. It is a practice of its own.

Reach Out

As you get closer to the top of some mountains, you might find yourself facing changing terrain. Loose rocks that will slide and fall as you step on them. Smaller and smaller ledges for you to walk across. Huge boulders you need to get yourself up and over. Or open slabs that leave you exposed to the elements. It's at this point where you will realize you can't finish the hike with just your two feet alone. You will need to reach out and use your hands.

Some hikes have tools built into them to help you with these parts. Ladders bolted against tall rocks you wouldn't easily be able to climb. Ropes and chains added to the spots where you might naturally try to pull yourself up. You might even bring walking poles to help steady yourself. But if the rocks and surfaces are easy enough to get over, you might just need to do a little scrambling—looking for a route where you can use your hands to help pull yourself up to the top.

When I was a kid, I used to think that if I had to use my hands in situations like this, I was doing something wrong. Not because it was wrong, but because I was looking at all the kids in my class who didn't seem to need to use their hands on the walks or hikes we did. The ones who jumped from rock to rock and raced up and down peaks and valleys with nothing but joy. I was too scared to get it wrong or hurt myself, which meant I didn't even try to do what they were doing. I just looked at how they moved around so effortlessly, and I instantly felt as though I wasn't good enough. I hated that I needed to use my hands and get dirty. I hated that I always felt as though I needed additional support. As I said in the beginning of this book, this often resulted in me just sticking to what I knew. Or worse yet, stopping partway through and waiting for everyone to finish.

Waiting meant that I spent a lot of time alone as a kid. Occasionally, someone would wait with me. But more often than not, I sat by myself and suffered in silence — all because I was afraid to try. I was afraid to see what my body could do. I was afraid to need the help. As I've gotten older, I have slowly (slowly, slowly, slowly) released these kinds of perfectionist tendencies. The more I walk and hike through this world, the more I've learned to appreciate the fact that my body is currently still capable of taking me where I want to go. And the more people I've met along the way, the more I've learned that we all need one another out there. We just need to have the courage to reach out. To use our hands, and to extend our hands to others. The same is true for opting out.

Letting go of your past self, and some of your past relationships, is not an easy process. It requires you to surrender to the unknown and accept that nothing lasts forever. And it might take years before you discover who you are, and what your life can be, on the other side. But I said this in my first book and I will say it again here: whenever you let go of something negative in your life, you make room for something positive — *if you are open to it.* You have to open your eyes and your heart and your life, and make space for new people to enter. You have to trust that you are worthy, and also that you have something to give. Because you are, and you do.

Before I got sober, the main way I connected with people was by doing drugs or drinking together. That's the only way I could show up and put myself into new situations. So it's sometimes strange for me now to think about how many new spaces and cities I've entered sober, and how many friends I've left with. It started with asking my friends if they wanted to go for walks or hikes rather than drink together. And that, along with a coffee or breakfast date, is the invitation that has continued to help me make friends ever since.

The thing about being nomadic is you have to try really hard to create a sense of home wherever you are. You can't just arrive in a city and expect to immediately be welcomed and integrated. You have to walk up to people and introduce yourself. In so many words, you have to ask if they want to be your friend. That's what I did in Cardiff. Before I arrived, I reached out to a friend from Instagram. Rachael is a wedding photographer in Wales, a wife, and the mother of three beautiful children. I saw all that online. But what I sensed through her photographs was that she loved the outdoors. So I messaged her to let her know I was going to be in the country for a while and asked if she wanted to go for a hike one day. She said yes. And with that, Adventure Tuesday was reborn in a new country.

In the first chunk of my time in Cardiff, Rachael and I had an adventure day almost every week. I would take the train to her town, she would pick me up from the station, and we would drive to one of her favorite spots. We walked all along the cliffs of the Gower Peninsula, found wild ponies at Rhossili Bay, and marveled at the turquoise waters alongside the crinkled coastline in Pembrokeshire. In the middle of each day, we would stop somewhere to eat a packed or pub lunch. Over sandwiches and cakes, we talked about our work, our thoughts on minimalism, and our family and friends. We shared similar tastes in television shows and got nostalgic listening to music we loved in our teens and early twenties. At some point, I told Rachael about the idea for this book. How I hoped it would help people feel a little less alone when they decided to carve out their own path in life. She nodded along and then said something I didn't expect to hear: "I think I'm used to being different now, because I'm Christian and most of my friends are not." My assumption must have been that there would be community in communion. And she did have community through her church, of course. But her beliefs made her stand out among many of the other people in her daily life. That didn't stop her from believing. It just made her different.

Rachael showed me a part of the country I never would've seen without her. She helped me fall in love with Wales. And after I returned from Paris, I was able to share those places with others. In September, I had reached out to two friends back home who I knew were thinking of coming to the UK in the fall. I let them know that if they had any interest in coming to Cardiff, I would love to host them—and they said yes. On October 27, I met Bre and Grady at the bus station, and we spent the next four days exploring Wales and North

Devon, in England. The first place I took them was Little Man because I wanted them to meet the people who took care of me almost every day. Then I showed them the places I loved, and we discovered a few new places together. We got a little lost and had to change some of our plans. But we navigated our adventures on the other side of the pond—and road—together, and made lifelong memories along the way.

The more I opt out and figure out what I value in life, the more people I seem to find who share similar values—but I have to look for them. And when I see them, I have to say something. I have to reach out and extend an invitation to connect. Because that's one of the most meaningful parts of this entire experience: finding people who seem to understand and support what you are doing. These people don't always need to become your best friends or be the people you constantly rely on, and you don't need to be that person for them either. That's a lot of expectation and pressure to place on a simple invitation, and nobody wants that, especially at the start. When you connect with other people who are opting out, you will find that you all have an inherent understanding that you might be on this journey together for only a little while. That doesn't mean it's not worth it. That means you should enjoy and appreciate all the time you get to spend together.

This is what the slope is, my friend. It's hiking your own hike and figuring out what you want your life to look like. Going back and forth with old stories that aren't serving you until you can finally let them go. It's the place where making decisions gets easier and easier. Where you're willing to let everyone go on their own journey too. And it's the place where

you're finding new people and building meaningful connec-
tions along the way. These are the steps, over and over again.
This is the final climb. There's no ultimate goal anymore.
You're doing all this because you want to, and because you
can. This is your life.

SECTION 5

The Summit

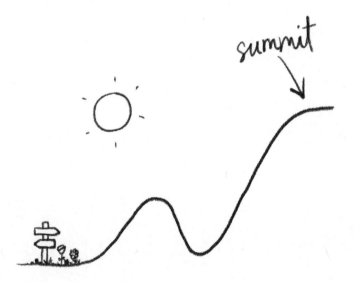

summit

When you finally reach the summit of a hike, it's obvious. You often find yourself surrounded by people, some quickly taking selfies and turning around to head back down, and others settling in to enjoy a break from their efforts. Everyone is smiling, riding high on what they have accomplished. And the view is extraordinary. This is the reason everyone is here; it's the reason you're here. And as soon as you took that last step up the slope of the mountain, you knew you had arrived.

The summit of an adventure in opting out is a little more subtle. In fact, if you aren't paying attention, you might even miss it. It's the moment the adventurous part of the journey is over, and you *are* who you set out to be. After months or years of staying on the wrong path, doing what you thought you should do or what was expected of you, you finally took the path less traveled—and now it's your own. You're no longer telling people that you're making a change or trying to live a different way. Here, you're at the point where you can simply say, "I am."

One of the reasons it's so important to talk about this kind of summit—and our often subtle arrival at it—is because it's the exact opposite of what so many self-help books suggest that the ending will look and feel like. I'm going to be honest and tell you that, instead of reaching a dramatic viewpoint, you might not always find a tangible "reward" at the end of this process. It's not about hitting a particular milestone or reaching a specific goal. So there likely won't be a moment that stands out as the one when you "did it." You took on the challenge and tried something new because you wanted to change your life. You wanted to live a different way. And now you do. *This* is what you wanted. *This* is the reward.

It could take you a long time to get here. In my experience, the length of time it takes to reach your summit depends on two things: how deeply ingrained the thing you opted out of is/was in your life, and if you have found personal fulfillment from your decision to walk away from it. When you choose to hike your own hike, you are always going to rub up against people who have chosen to stay on the path you left behind. And until you are truly content with your decision to step off it, you won't be fully at peace with your choice.

After I stopped drinking, it took me more than six years to finally be completely comfortable with this part of myself. To be fine with the fact that it meant some friends would leave me out of plans or leave me behind altogether, and some men wouldn't want to date a woman who is sober. And to also be fine with the fact that there are certain experiences I will never have. After six years or so, I stopped caring. Because I like my sober life. I like that I get to see the whole world through clear eyes now, and that I will remember everything I see and do. I even like that I have to feel all my feelings. That I have to sit in the discomfort of situations that I used to be able to get through only after applying a little numbing. I am better for it, and my life is better for it. Because for as many difficult feelings there are to feel, there are also so many wonderful ones. Moments of joy and elation that I wouldn't have experienced unless I was sober for them. I wouldn't trade this aspect of my life. It took a long time for me to say that, but it's true. I genuinely want to be sober forever. The "day" I reached the summit of that adventure wasn't memorable. It wasn't even a day. I just noticed I didn't care what anyone thought about my sobriety anymore. But it took me a long time to get there, because drinking was the way I connected with people — men, specifically — for fourteen years.

As for long-term travel, I don't actually know that I've reached the summit yet. I'm comfortable with my choice, and not worried about what I will miss out on by living this way. But part of me thinks that every country I choose to temporarily live in is going to come with its own adventure. There will be some initial concerns to work through, viewpoints that make me glad I went, a dip into at least one valley, and a slope to climb and make sure my time there is spent how I wish. So I don't know if there's a summit for life, so to speak. I can't tell you how long I will travel and live this way. But there was definitely a little summit in Wales that showed me I had done what I set out to do.

Be Where Your Feet Are

When you first start hiking, everything about it can feel like a struggle. Your first steps up. The new terrain. The dust and dirt. The sweat. And when it's a struggle, it's easy to switch from an adventurous mindset to one where you just want to finish and go home. So then your goal changes, and all you want to do is get to the top. When you get there, all you want to do is hike back down to the base and say you're done. You push yourself up and down, and you complete the hike — but you don't actually notice your surroundings or enjoy any of it. This is what happens when you're not living in the present.

Sadly, this is a mindset that Western society has cultivated and instilled in many of us: the idea that we always need to be thinking about what's next. What the next goal is, what the next milestone is, what the next measure of success is. Which hike we want to cross off the physical or metaphorical list. What you'll do if any of these things don't go according to plan. And you can apply the idea to all areas of your life. Work. Health. Relationships. Money. Hobbies. We're always moving the notch one step ahead and at a slight incline, thinking the only way forward is up. Next, next, next. More, more, more. Up, up, up. We are so focused on making linear progress that we lose sight of what's in front of us and we are never really here. I didn't realize I was doing the exact same thing toward the end of my trip to the UK.

In November, I moved back to the flat I had stayed in during my first six weeks in Cardiff and immediately fell into my old routine. I would wake up in the morning, pack my bag, and walk 1.5 miles to the coffee shop. I would write until midafternoon, walk 1.5 miles home, cook dinner, read, relax, sleep. And every week or two, I would text Rachael to ask which day she was free to go on our next hike.

As the days went on, I began worrying about how I would feel in December. I didn't know what I wanted to do after I left Wales, or who I would be able to see before I left the UK. And I still hadn't booked a flight home for the holidays, but I knew I had to pick a date sooner rather than later, before prices went up. There was still so much I wanted to do in Wales, and I was feeling something I'd felt on only a couple of trips before this one: homesick before I had even left. I couldn't find a word to properly explain this, but I was already anticipating how sad I was going to feel when I left the country. I didn't want to go.

I was sick for a couple of days that month and opted not to go to Little Man. But the day I returned, I walked through the front door and my favorite barista, Beth, announced "Cait's here!" loudly enough for everyone to hear. It was such a kind and simple statement. Both a greeting and a fact. But even in its simplicity, those words felt *big*. Because I *was* there. Temporarily living in Wales. I had set up a home and had a routine and had started friendships and created an actual life there. I didn't know what December would look like, or what I would do in 2020 or 2021 or any year after that. And I couldn't know. But what I did know was that I was there. I had left Squamish to see if I could live abroad and I had done it. I don't think that had really sunk in until Beth made the announcement. But if I look back, I can now see the sign that would've signaled that I was on the summit: it was my *routine*. The fact that I even had one in a new country meant I had done what I originally set out to do.

I have a long history of worrying about the future — something I'm sure you've noticed by now. So I am still always trying to calm this anxious mind of mine. It happened numerous times throughout 2019, and not just at the end of my travels. The first therapist I ever worked with used to notice it when we went for our walks. She would ask me questions, and I could never just come up with simple answers. My responses always went two, three, five, or ten steps ahead — to scenarios that might never happen. At the same time, my heart rate went up and I started holding my breath, gasping for air between run-on sentences. In four months of working together, the best thing she ever said to me was on one of those walks: "As you're talking, pay attention to how the ground feels beneath your feet." It was her way of helping me get out of my head and into my body. Better summed up as "Be here."

I know that parts of your adventure in opting out will be a struggle. But my hope is that you eventually get to a place where you're not thinking about it anymore. And then suddenly it hits you. And you realize you're doing it — you're living life on this new path. Don't rush through this moment. It's okay if it doesn't come to you at the exact minute you might have "reached" the summit. If you don't have a lot of practice living in the present, you probably won't see it right away, and that's okay. In fact, be prepared that it could take days or weeks or even months for it to dawn on you that you did the thing. You opted out. Walked off one path and walked down another. And it's not a struggle anymore. It's just part of you now. The people who practice living in the present always seem so calm, probably because they know that it's not about the destination. It was never about reaching the summit for you either. It was about creating a new way of life.

Whenever this realization comes to you, don't jump to the next goal or the next opt-out. And don't worry if you can't see what's ahead. Nobody can. Just be here. Stand right where you are and feel the ground beneath your feet. Then ask yourself a few questions. *How does it feel to be here right now? What does your life look like? Who have you met along the way? Who has helped you or impacted your life in a new way? Who or what have you lost? What have you given up to make this possible? What have you gained? Why has it been worth it?*

You don't have to wait until you get to the other side to answer these questions, by the way. You don't have to reach a specific milestone. You can just check in with yourself at any point throughout your journey. Then, when you're ready, you can do the next fun thing: celebrate how far you've come.

Celebrate

One of my favorite things to look for is how people celebrate reaching the summit of a mountain. If you watch, you might see friends splitting a snack or sharing a drink. They might also take a selfie, or get someone else to take a picture of them in a certain pose. These could look like simple everyday things that anyone might do at the top of a mountain—the snacks, the drinks, and the pictures. But if you ever talk to hikers about why they were doing it, you might find that these little actions have actually become their celebratory rituals.

Because we are always looking ahead for the next goal to achieve, we don't often celebrate our progress or successes along the way. You might tell yourself there's no time, or that you haven't done enough—or made enough progress—to celebrate yet. As a Canadian, I also tend to think we are just too modest to celebrate. And sadly, one story I used to tell myself was that I wasn't worthy of it.

One of the problems I see in this is that we have the wrong idea about what a celebration should be. We seem to think it needs to be big or loud. But those expectations are too high. I would never want to celebrate and create new rituals that way. But I do want to celebrate because I have also seen—and experienced—how good it feels to be able to look back and remember what I've accomplished. You've walked thousands of tiny steps and done so much work to get this far and to create the life you want. I want you to remember the moment you finally felt that to be true.

When I've asked friends if they have done anything to celebrate milestones in their opt-out journeys, not everyone said yes. But the ones who did celebrate did everything from cook a meal, to go out on a date, to buy themselves something they needed or wanted to keep going on this particular adventure, to book a vacation just for fun. A real mix of big and small stuff! My favorite celebratory ritual, though, came in the form of a ball of fried dough.

I wouldn't describe my friend Sarah as a typical opt-outer as we've been discussing them so far. She has a solid career as an accountant, eats and drinks basically everything, goes on one vacation per year, wants to get married and have kids, and so on. She is on a fairly conventional path in that regard, and she has happily chosen it. I would also describe her as an extremely experienced hiker. Sarah is the adventure partner you would want to take into the backcountry if you decided to venture out there. She spends a lot of her spare time planning physical adventures in the outdoors, and she has hiked some of the highest accessible peaks in the western United States.

Before every single hike, Sarah goes to the same coffee shop and buys herself one Boston cream doughnut. Then she takes the bag it's in, puts it at the top of what's inside her backpack, and begins her ascent. When she gets to the top, she opens the bag to see what she will find. You might be wondering, *Isn't there just going to be a doughnut in the bag?* Well, what you need to remember is that Sarah is someone who hikes at fairly high elevations—the lowest altitude being probably 11,000 feet above sea level, the highest being closer to 14,500. And the higher you go, the less air pressure there is. Sarah jokes that she eats a doughnut because the carbohydrates are important when you're that high up—and she's not exactly wrong about that. *Healthy* carbs do help you keep going and can also help prevent altitude sickness. But she gets a cream-filled doughnut because she knows there's a possibility that it could expand and explode in the bag. She packs it, therefore, not just so she can have a treat at the summit. She packs it because she enjoys hiking with the suspense of wondering what kind of mess she will find when she gets there, and she only laughs if she has to dig into the bag and get her hand dirty.

When Bre and Grady came to visit me in Wales, we created a little ritual like this of our own. At the end of every adventure we went on, we ate a baguette with some cheese and jam. That might not sound like much, but it was the messiness of our shared meal that was so fun. We typically didn't have a knife or spoon or anything that could help us turn these three ingredients into sandwiches. Instead, we took turns ripping off pieces of baguette with our hands, pulling off chunks of cheese, and dipping the combination into the jam. By the end of each meal, our hands were sticky, the ground beneath our feet was covered in crumbs, and we were licking our fingers and laughing.

With opting out, I do have a celebratory ritual. I've never

shared it with anyone before, partially because it's so small that it seems a bit silly. You might even think it's childish. But I did it once, without thinking it would ever be something I did again. And then the next time I hit a milestone that I felt should be celebrated, I remembered what I had done the last time and I did it again. And again, and again, and again.

It started in May 2013, on the day I made my final debt repayment. The way I officially decided to celebrate was by buying myself a coffee and taking it down to the beach. A drink enjoyed at a place that I loved and that afforded me a view. While I was at the beach, however, I did something I hadn't planned. Sitting on a piece of driftwood, I reached down and drew a smiley face in the sand. Two lines for the eyes and a curve for the smile. That was it. A simple smiley face that made me, in turn, smile when I looked down at it.

I repeated this ritual a little over two years later, after I finished the shopping ban. In the weeks leading up to the end, everyone asked me if I was going to buy myself something afterward. If I was going to "treat myself." The answer was no. I got to the end of that first year and knew I didn't need anything. I also knew I was going to carry on and do it for another year. But on the day I finished the shopping ban, I did go to the same coffee shop down the street and, this time, asked them to make me whatever they wanted. The barista filled my travel mug with something that was too sweet, but that felt like a celebration in its own right. Then I took my mug down to the same beach, sat on a piece of driftwood, and drew another smiley face in the sand.

I've repeated the smiley face part of this story in a few different places around the world. When I felt as though I was nearing the end of my big road trip around the U.S. in 2016, I drew one in the dust on the summit of Bishop Peak in San Luis Obispo, California. When I accepted the deal to write this book for Little, Brown Spark, I was finishing a hike down the mountain near my dad's house. I stepped off the path so I could hide behind a tree and cry. I called Emma with the news, tears of joy streaming down my face. Then I drew a smiley face in the dirt. These were little moments that wouldn't have looked or felt like anything to anyone else, but they were big moments when I realized how far I had come. I had set out to do a thing, and I knew I had done it.

The day Beth announced that I was at Little Man was the day I knew I had created a life for myself in Wales. This is exactly what I had hoped long-term travel would feel like. When I first thought about traveling, I didn't know this was going to happen in Wales, but it did—and I was glad for that. Later that afternoon, I went up to the counter and asked Beth and Gareth to make me any drink they wanted—a shock to their ears, as I must have ordered about a hundred oat lattes by that point. A few minutes later, Gareth brought over a little glass filled with ice, coffee, a splash of ginger beer (I think?!), and a sprig of peppermint. It was a little odd-tasting but surprisingly refreshing. When I was done, I lifted the glass off the table and found a ring of water from the condensation. Without thinking twice, I dipped my finger in the water and drew a smiley face inside the ring.

While I'm still not great at accepting compliments or celebrating some of the bigger milestones in life, I have grown quite fond of this private little ritual of mine. This isn't the kind of celebration that I would ever think to tell people about because it's so simple. It means something to only me. But it's precisely because it means something to me that I remember it. And I remember every single one of the places I have drawn smiley faces around the world—especially the one I drew in water on a table at a coffee shop in Cardiff.

Packing Out

There is a lot of material out there on how to pack *for* different adventures. Day hikes, backpacking trips, weekend getaways, trips around the world. A quick search on the internet will help you find all the tips you could possibly need on how much to pack, what gear you need and don't need, which bags to use, what airports allow for, and so on. It's interesting to me, then, that you can't find much information on how to pack *out*. We're so focused on what to bring that we don't think to talk about what you do with your stuff when the journey is over.

One of the pieces of trail etiquette I shared with you in the Viewpoint section was to pack out what you pack in. If you're going to spend time in nature, respect it—and the animals and people who will use it after you leave. So whatever you bring with you into the outdoors, take it home and dispose of it correctly there. That's easy, and it's something I've thought a lot about how to apply to travel as well.

So much of what is purchased before a trip, and during it, eventually becomes waste. We buy specific vacation clothes and toiletries. The clothes are often so cheap that they last for only that one trip, and the toiletries are so small that after a few uses they are thrown into the trash. We also leave room in our bags, or even bring bigger bags, so we can buy things on vacation and bring them home—much of which ends up being put into storage, or given to friends and family who don't really want it. What I'm saying isn't meant to make anyone feel bad. It's to start a conversation around how much waste we create by following the societal norms (a path!) about what travel looks like—and how inconvenient those little conveniences really are.

Thanks to the shopping ban, I changed my life and finances, which made it possible for me to be more nomadic. But in changing my shopping habits, I also changed how much waste I create in this world. I became intimately aware of how much stuff I had bought and barely used in the past, and I am not willing to make that same mistake again in the future—especially not to the detriment of other people or the planet. So it won't surprise you to know that I don't buy anything before a trip unless it is deemed absolutely essential (like a travel adapter for a different country). I tend to pack light—not because I'm a "minimalist," but because I really don't own that much stuff anymore. And I have a few reusable containers to pack toiletries in so I can lessen my impact in that area too. My goal is to use everything I bring and to then bring everything I've taken back home with me.

This falls under one of the other goals/values I set for long-term travel, which is to leave every place better than I found it. And this looked different every day. As an example, the one thing I didn't love about Cardiff was how much garbage was visible on the streets. As the weeks went by, I eventually started picking it up—especially if it was by the water. I didn't pick it up because I thought that act alone would make any difference. I know that collecting five or ten pieces of trash each day isn't going to do much in the grand scheme of things. I just couldn't continue walking past it and ignoring it. I saw something I didn't like and I couldn't unsee that. So I picked a little bit up each day. It wasn't much, but it was enough.

Sometimes leaving a place better than you found it can be even simpler than that. Consider cleaning up spills on a counter at a coffee shop even if you're not the one who made the mess. Or tidying up a home or hotel room you're staying in rather than leaving it all for the person who is going to come in and clean up after you. Making your host a cup of tea. Holding the door open. Lending a hand. Lending an ear. Lending your time. Offering words of gratitude and support. And treating everyone you meet like an old friend. When you're at home, plugged into your daily life, it's so easy to slip into a mindset where you get upset if anything disrupts your routine. It's easy to think it's all about you. But because opting out often leaves you standing on your own, it teaches you that the kindest thing we can do is take care of one another out there.

One of my favorite ways to "give back" probably can't even be described as that. It's more like a way to share what I have. When I'm done reading a book, I will typically leave it in a public place. Usually in a Little Free Library. If I can't find one, I will leave it on the chair of a coffee shop, or on a train, or anywhere else it will be protected from the elements. I bought and left probably more than a dozen books around Cardiff in my time there. I would often leave them on a bench at Little Man, usually with an inscription telling people to "enjoy and share!"

The more time I spent at Little Man, the more I learned about the staff who worked there and some of the ways they all gave back to their community. But it wasn't until my last week in Cardiff that a friend told me something I didn't know about the coffee shop. "Have you ever donated a coffee?" he asked. Not knowing what he meant, I went straight to the source and discovered Little Man's community initiatives, which I had never known about. Over the months, I had noticed that there were mornings when the homeless (or "sleeping rough," as they refer to it in Wales) community was welcomed in for free coffee and snacks. The space was also given to refugees and recent immigrants so they could meet to discuss how they were settling, finding work, et cetera. I had been coming in for months but learned only on my way out that I could apparently donate a few pounds so someone could enjoy a coffee during one of these events.

So much about my time in Wales had changed me and my outlook on life and the future. This country owed me nothing but had given me so much. I was the lucky one. I learned some tough lessons there too, but the staff at Little Man took care of me during all of it. They had become my family. And a line I've never forgotten from Elizabeth Gilbert's book *Eat, Pray, Love* is that "we must take care of our families wherever we find them." So on my last morning in Cardiff, I brought in a copy of my first book for the staff, along with a card. In the card I had enclosed my weekly Little Man budget in cash. I wrote that they should put the money toward one of their initiatives, and I had included a few words that would remind me of them forever: "A little man is still a man."

I have come to learn that living an intentional life might start as a solo journey but it never ends that way—or it shouldn't. If you are one of the fortunate people who gets to decide how you want to live your life, I believe it is only fair that you share that privilege in some way. Maybe that means you find a cause to donate your time or money to. Maybe it means you lift others up. Maybe it just means that you shine a light on this new path you've created for yourself, in hopes that others see that they might be able to create their own new path. It doesn't have to cost anything to be a better person, or a kinder person, or to be more open or honest. But in the same way that Brooke described how energy begets more energy, I think caring begets more caring. And when you care more, you see more. And when you see more, you can't unsee it. You have to act.

In thinking about the friends of mine who have opted out in their own ways, I can tell you they have all become better members of their individual communities since they started living more intentional lives. I didn't actually ask any of them about this. I've just witnessed it. I have watched them become activists for causes that matter to them, whether this means adopting more animals, raising money for charities and friends, making sure everyone they work with gets paid fairly, or moving their investments into socially responsible accounts. I didn't ask them about these things because these are not personal achievements. They aren't doing it for accolades or praise. They are doing these things because it aligns with their values. And the more they try to live in accordance with their values, the more capacity they seem to have to give.

Before I started packing up to leave Cardiff, I took a few more books from my pile and went for a walk so I could leave them in random places around the city. Then I squeezed the rest of my belongings into my 40L backpack, along with two books I wanted to keep: the copy of *The Confession* by Jessie Burton that I had bought at Shakespeare and Company in Paris, and a copy of *The Dutch House* by Ann Patchett, which I had bought in Cardiff. Two of my favorite reads from the whole year, and ones that I would always look at and remember fondly.

When I sat down on the train to London the next day, I felt exactly how I had anticipated I would: sad and already homesick. There was still so much I wanted to do in Wales. So many places I wanted to explore, and friendships I wanted to build upon. I wasn't ready to go. Curled up in the window seat, watching the green landscapes go by, I wasn't sure if I had left Wales better than I found it. I think it helped me more than I could ever help it. But I did the best I could at the time, and that's all we can ever ask of one another—and ourselves. All I could do now was take this version of myself back home.

Looking Back

You will never really know what a hike is going to look or feel like before you begin. Even if you have studied the trail websites and reviews and you think you have an idea of what to expect. It's impossible to know all the little things you will find along the path, or to know what you'll be able to do, until you get out there and see for yourself. Similarly, you can't know where your new path is going to take you at the beginning. But now that you're here—whatever "here" is or feels like to you—you know. You also know what it took for you to get here. And you know that you never could have predicted this is where you would end up. Drawing your own map is hard. You can't do it at the start. It's only after walking down a new path that you can look back and connect the dots. Eventually, you found your way and created a different life for yourself in the process—and now you can look back and see that the route you took makes sense.

I'm not surprised I spent 2019 trying to travel long term. Or that I tried, "failed," and then tried again. This is how so many of my opt-outs have gone. Looking back, I can see that I was slowly working my way toward this way of life for years. In 2018, I finally had the courage to fly over to Europe and navigate three new countries by myself. Before that, I had booked an Airbnb in Squamish and gone there for two months to see if I liked it—and then ultimately moved there. In 2016, I went on a road trip around the United States by myself for seven weeks. In 2015, I went on a road trip from Massachusetts to Virginia with my friend Sarah for ten days. In the years before, I had traveled a lot for work and gone to conferences around Canada and the U.S. on my own. And I had been on maybe half a dozen weeklong vacations throughout those years too. Making the decision to travel long term was scary in the moment. Looking back and connecting the dots, however, I can now see that I had always been building up to this—ever so slowly opting out of the stories that told me I couldn't travel and deciding to try anyway.

It's the same way I had always been building up to being nomadic. I think I have lived in six different cities—seven, if we include Cardiff—and at least twenty different homes. Looking back, every single one of my moves makes sense and feels like one of the many steps it took to get me here. It all makes sense. I am more comfortable when I'm moving around because I have always been in motion. My mom and I moved all the time when I was a kid. I grew up learning how to pack, unpack, settle in, and make friends. Then she met my dad, who was gone half the year, sailing with the Canadian Coast Guard. Through that, I learned how to communicate with someone who was away, and how to maintain long-distance relationships. So when people ask how I have friends all around the world, I think part of the answer is that this is all I've ever known.

Looking Back

Before I left Canada, I was struggling to understand if this way of life could ever work for me because I didn't know anyone else who had done it. I couldn't look to my family and find anyone who had ever lived exactly as I do today. If I had looked more closely at our family history, though, I would've seen that a lot of my relatives had opted out in their own ways. My mom moved across the country, to Victoria, in her early twenties. For her work, my aunt moved to a small town of fewer than two thousand people on the central coast of BC. Another aunt lived on a sailboat for most of her twenties. My dad, through his work, has lived on a boat for almost half his life. Two of my aunts chose not to have children. My dad quit drinking in his thirties. And my sister, who is so different from us all, never wavers in her decisions no matter what we think of them. I didn't see this at first because the stories I was told growing up didn't line up with these images. My family didn't tell me to do what they did and make lots of mistakes. They told me what they *wanted* for me. They wanted me to succeed, which is what I imagine most older generations want for those who come after them. So they pointed me to the safe paths. The paths that had clear steps and made sense to them. Where their advice was misguided was in thinking that the safe path was the right path. By shaking off their stories and taking my own path instead, I hope I am reminding them that you can't "succeed" on your own terms without stumbling and falling a few times first.

So what if we didn't grow up hiking or traveling? In the end, my family set me up and taught me everything I need to know to be a person in this world. How to walk and bike and swim. How to put one foot in front of the other and use my hands to lift myself up, and others too. How to move around

219

and create community wherever I go. How to be kind and generous. How to be honest. And most importantly, when I really look at the way they have all lived, they taught me how to try. These are skills and qualities I will have for life, and they will help me in all my future adventures.

I don't yet know what my future opt-outs will be. But again, I can look back and see that I'm able to live the way I do now only because of all the opt-outs I've done in the past. Deciding not to use drugs anymore. Getting out of debt. Changing my relationship with shopping. Leaving the public sector to work in the private sector. Leaving the private sector to work for myself. And quitting drinking—which taught me everything I would need to know in order to opt out of everything else since. Quitting drinking taught me how to listen to myself. How to do what was right for me. How to stand alone in a crowded room. How to feel my feelings. How to trust that I was resilient and could figure out how to deal with any situation I found myself in. How to build more meaningful relationships. How to be self-aware. How to express myself. And how to let others express themselves too. I couldn't travel the way I do today if I hadn't changed paths and changed my life in all those ways. It might have taken nearly ten years of opting out for me to get here. But it's not a race. It should never be a race. All that was time well spent.

Other than my dad's house, I have never lived anywhere for longer than two years. I used to feel a little bad about that, or worry what other people would think of me. There were so many stories in my head about people who "couldn't settle down," as well as the theory that travelers would "have to figure things out eventually." Some people might look at me and think those things, but that doesn't matter anymore because the only people who would think those things don't actually know me. This is who I am. I always have been. And I'm done thinking that I need to change and fit into a neatly labeled box.

There's a reason you've been thinking about making this change in your life. The answer might go back even farther than you think, and it might have been pushed down inside you with stories that told you not to take a different path. Maybe you can't look to anyone else and see where your new path might lead you. And maybe nobody will understand at the start what you're trying to do. But that doesn't mean you shouldn't do it. If you look back far enough, I bet you will find that someone in your family or past opted out in their own way. Or created their own path. Or has passed down skills or qualities that will help you on your journey.

When you look back and connect the dots, your adventure might not look exactly like the one I've outlined in this book: with one viewpoint and one valley and one final push up to the summit. Your adventure could look more like the reading of a heart rate monitor. Or maybe it won't be up and down at all. Maybe your adventure will be more like a mess of squiggles or circles, filled with more twists and turns than peaks and valleys. I don't know. The only thing I can guarantee is that progress is never linear. Your map won't be a straight line—and you will be better off for that.

Your Other Lives

So, what happens if you don't opt out? If you ignore the signs and whispers and continue to believe the stories that tell you to live a certain way? If you let your fear outweigh your excitement forever? If you decide not to follow your curiosity? What happens if you choose to stay on your current path? (Aside from living with the pain of ignoring the whispers, which will probably become internal screams.) The first and most obvious answer I can give you here is that the way you move through this world will essentially stay the same. You will continue to make decisions the same way you have up to this point, and you'll do things the way you've always done them. And I know I said this earlier, but maybe that's fine. Maybe you could have a fine life. You might even have a good life, or better yet, a great life. I'm not here to say that opting out is the best way to live. I am saying that it is one way to live. One path to choose. But you can absolutely choose to stay on the one you're on.

If I had stayed on some of my old paths, here is where I might be today.

I might have married one of my ex-boyfriends. We might have had two kids together, and bought a house in Victoria, and stayed in that city forever. I probably would have kept working for the government, and stayed working there for thirty-five years so I could collect my full pension one day. Then we would have retired and maybe traveled a little bit. We would have gone on tropical vacations, not because we necessarily wanted to but because that's what our friends did. When we were home, we could have picked up our grandkids from school and watched them for our kids. That might have been okay.

In another life, I might have bought the condo I was looking at when I was twenty-two years old. Instead of backing out of the deal at the last minute, I might have bought it and lived in it for five or ten years. I probably would have sold it when the real estate market was up, made a decent profit, and used that to put a down payment on my next home. Or used it to buy an investment property. Maybe real estate would have become my side hustle. Maybe I could have bought one property, then another, then another, and rented them all out or turned them into Airbnbs. I think it's safe for me to assume that I would have kept my stable government job to be safe. But maybe I would have become a real estate investor on the side rather than a writer. Financially, it probably would have paid off.

I'm sharing these hypothetical situations with you because these are two scenarios that were painted for me, through stories and suggestions from family and friends and society. They are great paths for some people, but they were not for me.

One of the most basic principles of personal finance is that everything is a trade-off. Unless you have an endless supply of money, you have to choose how you want to spend, save, and invest. And for every financial choice you make, you're also choosing *not* to spend, save, or invest in other things. We can't have it all or do it all. We have to make choices. The same goes for how we live our lives. You can't have it all or do it all in one lifetime. And there is a cost to staying on one path, especially if it doesn't feel like the one you should be on. But there is also a cost to walking away and venturing into the unknown. The real question is, *What price are you willing to pay?*

If I stick to my current path, here is what I could miss out on.

It's likely that I won't settle down somewhere — or won't choose a place to settle in until I'm entering my more senior years, if I'm lucky enough to see them. For that reason alone, I may never own a home. And I probably won't get married or have kids, which means I may never get to experience what it means to be a wife or a mom.

Some of these outcomes were once decisions I was scared to make. Some I didn't even know I was allowed to make. I had always just *assumed* I would get married and have kids. Then one day I realized I had a choice. I could choose to get married or not get married, and I could choose to have kids or not have kids. I could choose which paths I went down. As of right now, I don't want to go down those two paths — and those decisions are intentional. There is a purpose behind each one. I am absolutely open to the idea of having a partner for life, but I am not at all interested in getting legally married, unless we are from different countries and it would help us be together. As for kids, I would rather be Auntie Cait! I know there are trade-offs, and I am willing to pay the price. So I could be sad that I'm going to miss out, or I can be grateful for the life I will get to live. I will choose to be grateful.

I'm a big fan of Cheryl Strayed's work, particularly her old Dear Sugar column (and later podcast of the same name). My favorite was her response to a man who called himself Undecided. Undecided wrote in to explain that he wasn't sure if he wanted to have kids or not. He could see himself being happy either way. He shared that he was exploring the ideas of what both paths might look like, and he asked Cheryl how one might decide—and how to not make a decision you will regret. The entire column (called "The Ghost Ship That Didn't Carry Us"), which is brilliant, could be summed up in her closing paragraph: "I'll never know and neither will you of the life you don't choose. We'll only know that whatever that sister life was, it was important and beautiful and not ours. It was the ghost ship that didn't carry us. There's nothing to do but salute it from the shore."

Coming Home

There's a certain sense of accomplishment you feel when you return home from a difficult hike. The high you felt at the summit slowly calms down and turns into more of a feeling of pride. Before, you didn't know if you could do it, but you proved to yourself that you can. It's not always a huge boost to the ego — it's usually a little softer than that. There's an understanding that you braved the elements, and perhaps even put yourself in a vulnerable position, and you managed it. You now know that you are capable of more than you imagined, and you return with shaky legs and a humble confidence.

One of the biggest reasons it can be difficult to change paths in life is because you have to give up pieces of your identity in the process. To challenge stories you have believed, or even let go of roles you've played for most of your life. To release parts of yourself you thought were true or wanted to be true. To step off one path you've been walking on and try taking a different one. As Colin Wright wrote in his book *Come Back Frayed,* "No one wants to start over, or risk starting over, in the pursuit of results that are anything but guaranteed. No one wants to walk paths that are less than certain, less safe, or less socially acceptable." But speaking from experience, I can tell you that the scariest part of the whole journey is the fear you will face before you even begin. If you can get through that, I have no doubt you'll be able to work through what comes next.

It's a beautiful thing, to allow yourself to evolve. To challenge yourself to grow and change. To even attempt to step into who you want to be in this world. Choosing to trust your gut and listen to the whispers telling you you aren't being true to yourself anymore is empowering. If you do it once, my guess is you will opt out of something else in the future. And the farther you go down this new path, the more you'll see that you weren't actually walking away from anything. You were walking toward yourself. That is a journey worth taking, even if you don't know how it's going to end.

Shortly after booking my return flight and leaving Wales, I still felt as though things were off with this whole adventure. I didn't feel good about some of the things I did that year. They weren't bad, but they didn't feel great—slightly out of alignment with my values. There's an exercise that Brooke outlines in her book *Slow,* where she suggests that you write your eulogy in just three sentences and try to live by those words. The idea had always stumped me before. I wasn't afraid of dying; I just had no idea what anyone would say about me. This time, after living out of alignment for part of the year, I knew what was missing—and as a result, I knew what I wanted people to say. I couldn't get it down to three sentences, but I wrote my eulogy in six. There was nothing overly specific in it. No goals, no achievements, nothing about the work I do. I wrote about the person I hope people remember me as. I drew my North Star. I'm sharing this because I need you to know that it took nearly ten years for me to figure this out. I didn't wait until I knew who I was before I attempted to live an intentional life. I attempted to live an intentional life in order to figure out who I was.

In an interview on the podcast *Oprah's SuperSoul Conversations,* Gloria Steinem said, "We are born who we are." I always felt as though I understood that about others, but 2019 felt like the first year that I could really understand what that meant for me. In 2019, I stepped into a lifestyle that I had waited years to try out. Not every action ended up aligning with my values, but every aspect of traveling itself felt natural to me. I don't just feel like my best self when I'm on the road. I feel like myself, period.

I've opted out enough times by now to know that when you leave the path you're on, literally or figuratively, you are going to come back to your life altered. In my earliest opt-outs, I thought you came back a different person. But what I realized after my 2019 travels is that you're still the same person. You already have everything you need inside you. You were always capable of doing the thing you set out to do. You just didn't know until you tried.

So I'm happy to report that the truer statement is also a little simpler. A little easier to imagine. A little less scary to consider when you're thinking of changing paths in life. Whenever you dare to go on an adventure, you will always come home a little more like yourself.

Conclusion

So you've seen the signs, or heard the whispers, and you know what you need to do. And now you've reached the trailhead. You're going to opt out of something. What is it? And why? The answers to these questions are going to vary greatly among everyone who reads this book. It's also true that your own answers will be different every time you pick it back up to remind yourself what the process and experience of opting out are going to entail. The same way there are countless hikes you can go on, there are innumerable ways you can live your life. So there are no right or wrong answers. Only old and new paths.

Don't be surprised if you notice that at first your answers come out like bullet points or factual statements. As if you have to justify why you're changing paths and outline your plan down to the very last detail. You've been conditioned to believe there's a reason you should be on your current path. This means you're going to have to unlearn some things and change the stories in your head—and it won't happen over-night! Your answers will shift again and again as you go down your new path and learn more about yourself. For now, you need only an answer that feels good enough to get you started.

It's probably also important to note that your answer to why you're doing it doesn't need to be complicated. In fact, please don't let it stress you out. It could be as simple as "Because I want to" (or don't want to, depending on the situation in question). In fact, I *hope* your answers are eventually that simple. Because nobody will understand when you don't have a clear reason. But they don't need to! If you need everyone to understand you or agree with you, you'll never be able to live a truly intentional life—because it won't be yours.

So, what do *you* want to do? Here is where I hope you'll give yourself the space to dream a little, as well as some time to reflect on the question. Sometimes you'll have a reason that "makes sense" to people. But there also doesn't need to be any good reason for what you do, aside from the fact that you want to do those things! When I left Squamish, I knew I wanted to spend most of 2019 in the UK. I didn't know why, and it's not where most of my friends would have chosen to travel. I just knew I'd seen a little bit of it and I wanted to see more. It was as simple as that.

So the answers are all yours. As an example, I have friends who don't drink because it has never appealed to them. Or they don't like the taste. Or they always got sick when they drank. Or they didn't have the money for it. Or they did have the money but felt as though it was a waste. Or they had an unhealthy relationship with it. Or they were alcoholics and had to quit. Or they knew that alcoholism ran in their family and they literally never had a single drop for that reason alone.

Likewise, I have friends who don't want kids because it never appealed to them. Or they don't like kids. Or they do like kids but just don't want their own. Or they don't feel they are in the financial position for it. Or they are in the financial position but want to do different things with their money. Or they are worried about bringing kids into the climate crisis.

It's safe to say the experience of opting out is a process of becoming more self-aware. To be self-aware, you have to know what you're doing and know how you feel about it. And if you don't feel good about it, you have to make a practice out of trying to realign with what feels right for you. By opting out of one thing, you're opting into yourself. And if you're anything like the friends I talked to for this book, you will continue to do this over and over again in the future.

For now, the only thing you have to do is decide which path you want to step off and which one you want to go down instead. You don't need to know where it's going to lead you or what the ultimate goal is. And you can't know that stuff anyway because there's no map or route marked out, and things don't always turn out like you may be anticipating at the beginning of a journey. Just step up to the trailhead. Remember that you don't have to be "good" at opting out. It's not about perfection. And it can't be! This path comes with entirely new territory that you'll need to learn how to navigate. All you can do is put one foot in front of the other and explore a new idea you have about the way you want to live. The first step is the hardest to take, but it's also the closest.

Epilogue

Before I decided to opt out of life in Squamish and attempt to travel long term, I wanted answers. I wanted to know what people would think. I wanted to know how it would impact my finances. I wanted to know if it would hurt my chances of dating. I wanted to know if it would work. I left and collected some of that data. My travels didn't affect my relationships much. If anything, some of them got even better thanks to what I learned that year. My finances were fine. And this opt-out wasn't particularly dramatic, which I'm grateful for. But despite the fact that 2019 was mostly drama-free, it taught me one of the most important lessons of my opt-out life: that I'm never going to have the answers. I'm never going to know where any path will take me or how it will work out. That doesn't mean it's not worth trying. It is absolutely worth trying. It just means that I'm never going to know what will happen.

If you're curious about my current thoughts on climate change and flying and travel in general and how they are going to shape my decisions in the future—well, I don't know that either. I did the best I could in 2019. I know that much is true. I also know it's true that individual choices won't have as big an impact as huge societal and systemic changes will. But there were still more than a few times when I felt as though I was living out of alignment with my values, and we know what that means: I need to look at it and figure out what's next for me personally. This is new territory for me to explore and learn about and test ideas on. I won't pressure myself to do it perfectly, just as I wouldn't expect perfection from anyone else. The only thing we can do is try to live in a way that feels true to us and allow others to do the same. So what I can say right now is, I'm thinking about it.

This wasn't the year I expected to have, nor the one I thought I would ever write about. But if I have learned anything throughout this entire process, it's that we can't write our futures. We can't write that we are going to do something with all certainty because it may not happen that way. We can only write our stories as they happen, or after we've lived and can connect some of the dots. To live an intentional life, then, you don't need to have your whole life figured out. Instead, all you have to do is have some purpose or reason behind every decision you make. It doesn't need to be a big "I'm going to change the world" kind of purpose. You can just do something because it feels right, or you want a challenge, or you want to learn something new. You can also do it just because you want to. And as things come up, keep trying to make intentional decisions along the way.

Maybe I'll never have another year when I travel quite as I did in 2019. Or maybe I'll carry on, and in five years I will look back and see that all of 2019 was the valley of this adventure. Maybe it was. Maybe that whole year was the messy middle of my attempt to be nomadic. There were certainly more things that came up along the way that I didn't include in this book. It was the year I started dating again. It was the year I learned how to have radically honest conversations. It was the year I removed my ego and tried to love people unconditionally, even if they hurt me. It was also the year I had my first real health scare of any kind. The year I had my trust and privacy deeply violated by someone I cared about. And the year I decided to go back into therapy. The most honest thing I can say about why I didn't include these stories is *because* they would've added only a dramatic effect. They had nothing to do with the adventure I was on. They were real-life situations. Things that could've happened anywhere and at any time, not specifically because I was opting out. And while the details might have made the story more interesting, they aren't helpful for *you* in the context of this book.

If I could go back and talk to the Cait who was scared to give up her apartment in Squamish, I would tell her to not take it all so seriously. In fact, I should have just opened up my high school yearbook from the year I graduated and read my write-up, because seventeen-year-old Cait had some very good advice back then. After declaring my supposed love for my high school sweetheart, I had written, *If you're lucky, you might get eighty-five years on this planet. Don't spend them living with regret.* I don't know where or how I got this insight at such a young age, but somehow I knew it then, and yet I *still* need to constantly give myself this advice today. Because the reality is that I don't know what I'm doing. I don't know if "experts" are supposed to say that, which is one of the reasons I don't want to be labeled as one. But it's true: I don't know. Maybe I'll travel more. Maybe I'll stop. Maybe I'll buy a place and settle down somewhere. Maybe I'll change my mind about marriage and kids. Maybe I won't. Maybe none of it really matters. I don't know, friend. I'm figuring it all out as I go, as I suspect you are too. If travel has taught me nothing else, it's that there are so many different ways to live, and so many different paths we can take. I hope I get to the end of my life and can say I took hundreds of them.

The only way to live without regret, then: do what feels right for you, and try not to hurt people along the way. Show up as yourself. Be honest. Be kind. Lend a hand. Lend your time. Ask questions. Learn. Focus on something or someone other than yourself. Figure out what feels wrong and actively try to make it feel right. This is all a recipe for living an intentional life. Don't be reckless, of course. But if you screw up and do feel as though you regret any of your behavior, apologize or try to fix it! Because that's the intentional thing to do too. But don't stress yourself out by thinking you need to do any of this stuff perfectly. You can't. It's impossible. Also, if you did it perfectly the first time, you wouldn't have learned anything. What's the point in that?

As for the question about whether or not you're going to lose people along the way? Well, you probably will. I have, and I'm sure I will lose more in the future. But if you're true to yourself and stick to your values, you will find some incredible new people — people you couldn't have imagined meeting, let alone being able to call your friend or partner one day. As for the ones you leave behind on your old path, you might miss them, or feel nostalgic for the time you spent together. In fact, there's a word in Welsh that could potentially be used to describe that feeling, although the word itself can't be fully translated: *hiraeth*. You might say it's the feeling of missing someone or something while being grateful for their existence. You might also use it to describe homesickness or a longing for a place you once visited. I think *hiraeth* is the word that could sum up how I was feeling before I left Wales. I carried it home with me, and I dream about returning to the country again soon. It's the same way I can miss the people I've lost in my life but still reminisce and feel grateful for the time we spent together.

I returned home from Wales on November 28, 2019 — almost one year from the date I had left Squamish. Aside from the worst jet lag I've ever had, it was a softer landing than my trip home from the UK in the spring. I was a little solitary at first, mostly because I was still completing the first draft of this book. But when I started getting together with friends, nobody made assumptions about what I was doing or told me I was missing out on anything by living this way. Instead, after nearly ten years of challenging myself to change paths and live differently, people asked me some form of the same question: "When's the next adventure?"

Acknowledgments

The original dedication for this book was *For every adventure partner who has held out their hand and helped me on my journey*. It felt more appropriate to list some of them here.

First, I have to say that this book exists only because a handful of people could envision what I wanted to create. In a way, its undertaking was an opt-out of its own. I proposed to write a book in a style I hadn't seen before and couldn't provide any clear examples of for comparison. Few people understood the idea, let alone trusted that the book would make any sense. But Little, Brown Spark could see the path I was already on and offered to help me carve out the next section of it. For that, I will always be grateful.

To my editor, Marisa: Your encouragement and support have meant more to me than I will ever be able to express. You helped me stay calm when I was in crisis and helped me step into myself as an author. Thank you for making me feel seen and heard throughout this process. I hope that what we've created together will help readers feel the same way.

To my agent, Lucinda: Your enthusiasm has always kept me

Acknowledgments

going, and I wouldn't be doing any of this without you. But what I'm most grateful for is how our friendship has grown in the time we've been working on this project. Thank you for crying with me.

To my friend, Shannon: Girl, what do I even say here?! You were the first person who truly understood what this book was going to look like and who it was going to help. Your belief in me helped me believe in myself. And there is no one else I would have trusted to read and help me edit the ugly first draft. Thank you for being my adventure partner in writing.

To my friend and talented illustrator and artist Amanda Sandlin: Thank you for bringing every idea I've had to life, starting with the cover of this book. Because of you, this project always felt more like a collaboration. I will always remember *AIOO* as something we did together.

To everyone I interviewed: Thank you for sharing your stories with me. We didn't include everyone or everything in this book. But your words helped me feel like I was on the right path and gave me the confidence to share this idea with the world.

Special thanks to some of the people who helped me in 2019. Fiona, for being an incredible host. Saima, for all our slow days. Jessica, for drawing me a bath. Bianca, for both the deep conversations and the laughter. Tom, for letting me show up as my full self. Kate, for coming down (twice!) to see me. Kara, for the trip of a lifetime. Chris Enns, for all our rambles. And Mimi, for Paris. Tiffany, for the late-night phone calls. Janine, for looking out for me. Paul, for being sweeter than you might think. Chris Bailey, for the flowers you didn't know I needed. Tammy, for always making time and sharing incredible resources. Derek, for continuing to be a mirror and supporting me after all this time.

Acknowledgments

Beth, for taking care of me at Little Man—even after I left Cardiff. Azalea, for holding space for me and teaching me how to ask for what I need. Pascal, Meg, Fiona, Rachael, and everyone else I had adventure days with. My family, for always welcoming me home, even when I come back changed. My beautiful friends in beautiful Squamish. And Emma, my best friend and the strongest woman I know.

Finally, to my online friends and community: I wouldn't be doing the work I am today if it wasn't for you. Thank you for being patient while I took time off to quietly work on this project and on myself. I am so excited to see where our conversations go from here.

Community

Hi, friend!

I want to thank you for reading this book of mine. *The Year of Less* felt like the book I was allowed to write, but *Adventures in Opting Out* is the book I *wanted* to write—an idea born on the trails of my backyard mountain that is now a piece of work you can hold, read, and listen to. I'm so grateful you decided to pick it up, and I hope it becomes a trusted guide you can carry with you on your journey.

Now that you're done, you might be wondering how you can find and connect with other readers and adventurers. It's safe to say we all know how important this can be while opting out, especially when we've all felt alone at least once. In the outdoors community, people will tell you to "leave no trace" of yourself on a path you've taken, and I firmly believe in this philosophy. But when it comes to opting out, I hope you will leave a *tiny* trace of what you're doing—and show us what it looks and feels like to be carving out your own path.

Giving myself permission to change paths in life—and to sit with the discomfort that comes with scaling the peaks and valleys — has been challenging. However, by honoring myself, making hard choices, and going after them intentionally (and imperfectly), I also know I've given permission to other people to do the same. You don't have to follow *my* path (and I think you know by now that you shouldn't). But I hope you'll tell at least one person what "adventures in opting out" means to you.

After the launch of *Adventures in Opting Out*, I'll be working on a podcast of the same name to go along with it. I have also compiled a list of additional resources — books, blogs, podcasts, people I love to follow — that you might enjoy. You can find all that at my website:

caitflanders.com/adventures-in-opting-out

Also, it probably won't surprise you to know that I've opted out of using certain social media platforms over the years. At the time of publishing this book, the best place to find me online is through Instagram (@caitflanders). Please feel free to say hi over there! And if you want to connect with others, add the hashtag #adventuresinoptingout to a post of your own and follow it so you can see what others are sharing.

Be kind and be safe out there. And remember that it's all an adventure.

xx Cait

Index

Index

Index

Index

Index

Index

Index

Index

Index

Index

About the Author

Cait Flanders is the author of the *Wall Street Journal* bestseller *The Year of Less*. Described by *Vogue* as "a fascinating look into a living experiment that we can all learn from," the book has been translated into eight languages. It went on to become one of the most sold nonfiction books on Amazon in July 2018 and one of Powell's Staff Top Fives that same year. Her story has been shared in the *New York Times, The Guardian,* the *Globe and Mail,* Oprah.com, *Forbes,* and more. Flanders always has an adventure on the calendar and believes in leaving every place better than she found it. She is from Victoria, BC, Canada.

caitflanders.com
Instagram: @caitflanders